for 3 - 9s

Book 3

CHRISTIAN FOCUS PUBLICATIONS

We believe that the Bible is God's word to mankind, and that it contains everything we need to know in order to be reconciled with God and live in a way that is pleasing to him. Therefore, we believe it is vital to teach children accurately from the Bible, being careful to teach each passage's true meaning in an appropriate way for children, rather than selecting a 'children's message' from a Biblical passage.

© TnT Ministries
29 Buxton Gardens, Acton, London W3 9LE
Tel: (020) 8992 0450

Published in 1997 by Christian Focus Publications Ltd.,
Geanies House, Fearn, Tain, Ross-shire IV20 1TW
Tel: (01862) 871 011   Fax: (01862) 871 699
www.christianfocus.com

Reprinted 2000

Cover design by Douglas McConnach

This book and others in the series can be purchased from your local Christian bookshop. Alternatively you can write to TnT Ministries direct or place your order with the publisher.

ISBN 1-85792-320-0

TnT Ministries (which stands for Teaching and Training) was launched in February 1993 by Christians from a broad variety of denominational backgrounds who are concerned that teaching the Bible to children be taken seriously. They have been in charge of the Sunday School of 50 teachers at St Helen's Bishopsgate, an evangelical church in the City of London, for 13 years, during which time a range of Biblical teaching materials has been developed. TnT Ministries also runs training days for Sunday School teachers.

CONTENTS
On the Way for 3-9s / Book 3

Preparation of Bible material:
Thalia Blundell
David & Christine James

Editing:
David Jackman

Illustrations:
Ben Desmond

Craft Activities:
Andrew Blundell
Thalia Blundell
Trevor Blundell
Sue Chapman
Annie Gemmill
Kathy Pierce
Sue Upcott

On the Way works on a three year syllabus. It covers the main Bible stories from Genesis to the Acts of the Apostles. All the Bible stories are taught as truth and not myth.

Each year the birth of Jesus is taught at Christmas, and the death and resurrection of Jesus at Easter. Between Christmas and Easter the syllabus covers aspects of Jesus' life and teaching, and after Easter there is a short series on the Early Church. The rest of the year is spent looking at the Old Testament stories, covering broad sweeps of Old Testament history. In this way leaders and children gain an orderly and cohesive view of God's dealings with his people throughout the Old and New Testaments.

The lessons are grouped in series, each of which is introduced by a series overview stating the aims of the series, the lesson aim for each week and an appropriate memory verse.

Every lesson, in addition to a lesson aim, has Bible study notes to enable the teacher to understand the passage, suggestions for visual aids and an activity for the children to take home. One activity is suitable for 3-5 year olds, one for 5-7 year olds and one for 7-9s.

How to Prepare a Lesson

To prepare a Sunday School lesson properly takes at least one evening (2-3 hours). It is helpful to read the Bible passage several days before teaching it to allow time to mull over what it is saying.

When preparing a lesson the following steps should be taken -

1. PRAY!

In a busy world this is very easy to forget. We are unable to understand God's word without his help and we need to remind ourselves of that fact before we start.

2. READ THE BIBLE PASSAGE

This should be done **before** reading the lesson manual. Our resource is the Bible, not what someone says about it. The Bible study notes in the lesson manual are a commentary on the passage to help you understand it.

3. LOOK AT THE LESSON AIM

This should reflect the main teaching of the passage. Plan how that can be packaged appropriately for the age group you teach.

4. STORYTELLING

Decide how to tell the Bible story. Is it appropriate to recapitulate on what has happened in previous weeks? Will you involve the children in the presentation of the story? What sort of questions are appropriate to use? How will you ascertain what has been understood? Is there anything in the story that should be applied to their lives?

5. VISUAL AIDS

What type of visual aid will help bring the story alive for the children? Simple pictures may be appropriate. For stories with a lot of movement it may be better to use flannelgraphs or suedegraphs. In some instances models may be appropriate, e.g. the paralysed man being let down through a hole in the roof. Do remember that visual aids take time to make and this will need to be built into your lesson preparation.

6. CRAFT ACTIVITIES

Many of the craft activities require prior preparation by the teacher so do not leave it until the night before!

Benefits of On The Way

- Encourages the leaders to study the Bible for themselves.

- Chronological approach gives leaders and children a proper view of God's dealings with his people.

- Each lesson has 3 age related craft activities.

- Everything you need is in the one book, so there is no need to buy children's activity books.

- Undated materials allow you to use the lessons to fit your situation without wasting materials.

- Once you have the entire syllabus, there is no need to repurchase.

Teacher's Challenge

Located throughout this book are cartoons highlighting some aspects of the Bible passages. Hidden in one or more of these cartoons is a bookworm (see box on right - not actual size).

If you consider yourself observant and want a challenge, count the number of times the bookworm appears in this edition. The correct answer is on the bottom of page 74. Don't look until you are sure you have found them all!

Jesus Teaches About Prayer

Week 1

THE LORD'S PRAYER   *Matthew 6:5-15*
To teach the important aspects of prayer.

Week 2

PERSEVERANCE IN PRAYER   *Luke 18:1-8*
To teach the importance of persisting in prayer, being certain that God will answer.

Week 3

HUMILITY IN PRAYER   *Luke 18:9-14*
To understand that we are able to draw near to God on the basis of what he has done for us, not what we have done for him.

Week 4

FORGIVENESS IN PRAYER   *Matthew 18:19-35*
To show that God expects us to forgive others in the same way that he has forgiven us.

Series Aims

1. To teach the children that prayer is as important as eating.

2. To teach the children how to pray.

This series looks at some of Jesus' teachings about prayer.

Week 1 deals with how we should pray (the Lord's Prayer) and week 2 with perseverance in prayer. Two extra lessons on attitudes of prayer are included for use when Easter is late.

Prayer, at its simplest, is talking with God. It is important for the children to realise that prayer is not something we do naturally, but is a response to God. Prayer can only occur if God has already touched that person's spirit. God does not, therefore, guarantee to hear every person's prayer (Isaiah 1:15; 29:13).

True prayer involves the recognition and acceptance of God's will in that situation, and is based on God's mercy and willingness to forgive rather than on our own good deeds.

Memory Work

The Lord's Prayer
Our Father in heaven,
Hallowed be your name,
Your kingdom come,
Your will be done on earth as it is in heaven.
Give us this day our daily bread
And forgive us our sins,
As we forgive those who sin against us.
And lead us not into temptation but deliver us from evil.
For yours is the kingdom and the power and the glory
For ever and ever.
Amen

(You may want to change the wording of the prayer to fit the one used in your church.)

Preparation:
Read Matthew 6:5-15, using the Bible study notes to help you.

Lesson aim:
To teach the important aspects of prayer.

6:5-7 They are told how not to pray. Prayer should not have the aim of impressing others, as with the hypocrites, nor is it to impress God through the use of endless words. Rather, prayer should express the relationship we have with a Heavenly Father who is aware of our needs (v.8) and will answer our prayers (v.6).

6:9 **Our Father ...** It is right to address God in this way because we are to look up to him in love and trust. He is the one who is always near us in perfect love. Also, 'our' indicates the unity of believers.

In heaven ... acknowledges God as the Almighty Ruler over heaven and earth.

May your name be honoured ... is a prayer that God will work in all people so that everyone will worship and serve him.

6:10 **May your kingdom come ...** The kingdom has two aspects - present and future. Firstly, that God may rule in my heart here and now and in the hearts of individuals all over the world. Secondly, that Jesus will come again, establishing God's kingdom for ever.

May your will be done ... In heaven God's will is gladly obeyed by everyone all the time. Believers should pray that the same will apply on earth now.

6:11 **Bread ...** symbolises everything we need for daily life. Linking this to the previous verses we see that we need daily food to enable us to do God's will. We look to 'our Father' to provide out of his great love for us all we need, so that we can live according to his will.

6:12 **Forgive us our sins ...** This is both a prayer and a confession. By praying for forgiveness we admit we have sinned. As we receive forgiveness from God we must also forgive others.

6:13 **And lead us not into temptation ...** If you have just prayed for forgiveness you long not to sin again. We confess here that we easily sin and plead with God not to allow us to be brought into situations which involve great temptation.

6:14-15 Failure to forgive is itself a sin. Thus true prayer to be forgiven must inevitably mean that we forgive others. If we do not, then our prayer cannot have been sincere.

Conclusion

We need to help the children understand that we can approach the God who is the maker of heaven and earth as our Father, but we must remember that he is the ruler of all. Therefore, our requests for ourselves should have the aim of loving and serving him better. It could be discussed with the children how they pray at home - do they just ask for things?

For teaching purposes this prayer can be split into 6 petitions - the first 3 dealing with God, the last 3 with me.

1. God's name
2. God's kingdom
3. God's will
4. My need of bread
5. My need of forgiveness
6. My need of victory

Lesson Plan

As this is the first lesson of the series, you need to start with an introduction. Tell the children that the group will write a letter to God. Ask the group to contribute things to go in the letter. When the letter is finished sign it and put it in an envelope. Ask the children where to address the letter. Can we send a letter through the post to God? How can we send our message to him? Can we telephone God? Explain that prayer is talking to God. Jesus taught his friends how to talk to God. Tell the children that Jesus started by telling his friends 2 things not to do when praying. Ask them to listen carefully so that they can tell you what the 2 things were.

At the end of the story go over the 2 things Jesus said not to do. Remind the children that God always hears them, even though they cannot see him. End with a short time of prayer, encouraging the children to pray one sentence prayers.

Visual aids

Work out from the passage the aspects you want to stress - e.g. privately (v.5-6)
simply (v7-8)
putting God first, etc.

For the 3-7s you will need pictures to illustrate these points.
- privately - a child praying on their own in a room.
- simply - 2 children praying. One has a speech bubble with a single line of speech, the other an enormous speech bubble with the same line of speech repeated many times.
- God first - the word 'God'.
- daily bread - a loaf of bread (or other staple food).
- forgiveness - a child being hugged by a parent.
- freedom from temptation - a child with back turned to a bar of chocolate or other desirable thing.

For the older ones you can use words.

Have a big heading on the board 'How to Pray' and pin up the pictures/words as you come to them. Talk about what each aspect means in the life of the child.

Take time to teach the prayer.

Activities / 3 - 5s

Photocopy page 8 for each child. Fold the page in half to make a card with the pictures on the outside. Prior to the lesson write inside each card **Just me**. Talk about the front of the card with the children, putting a tick or cross in each box. (Each box should end up with a cross!) At the end, stress that the children only need themselves to pray to God. They can draw a picture of themselves above the words 'Just me'. The cards can be coloured if time permits.

Activities / 5 - 7s

The children will make a prayer flower. Follow the instructions on page 9.

Activities / 7 - 9s

Photocopy page 12 onto white paper and page 13 onto coloured paper for each child.
- Cut out the hand from the sheet of white paper, cutting around the outer edge of the black line.
- Cut along the solid lines around the 4 windows and fold back along the dotted lines.
- Put glue around the outer strip of the hand on the sheet of coloured paper where marked. Place the cut-out hand on top, being careful to line up the flaps with the words underneath. Press firmly around the edges of the hand to secure it.
- Punch 2 holes at the top of the sheet of coloured paper and thread a length of wool through them to make a wall hanger.

Space Tours Ltd.

How to pray

What do I need to talk to God?

Each child requires pages 10 and 11 photocopied on card and this page photocopied on yellow paper, a dowel or garden stick approximately 30 cm long, glue and sellotape.

Instructions

- Cut out both large circles and glue the yellow circle containing the words of the Lord's prayer onto the centre of the card circle.
- Cut out the 5 small circles and colour, leaving the words visible.
- Cut the small circles in half to make petals and glue them around the edge of the large card circle on the back. Alternate blank and word petals. Make sure the petals do not overlap too much.
- Attach the dowel or garden stick to the back of the large card circle with sellotape to make a stem.

The Lord's Prayer

Our Father in heaven,
Hallowed be your name,
Your kingdom come,
Your will be done on earth as it it in heaven.
Give us this day our daily bread
And forgive us our sins,
As we forgive those who sin against us.
And lead us not into temptation but deliver us
from evil.
For yours is the kingdom and the power and the
glory
For ever and ever.

Amen

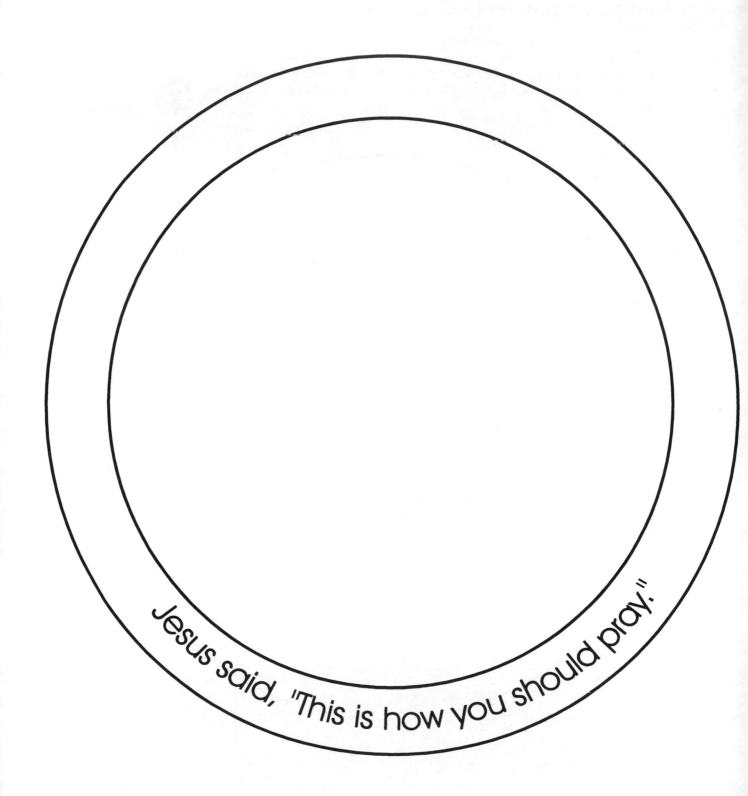

Jesus said, "This is how you should pray."

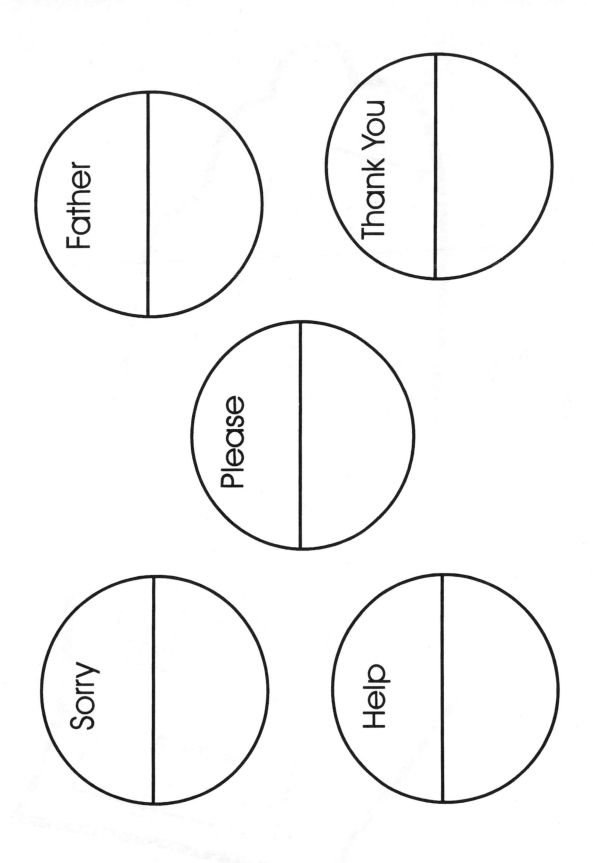

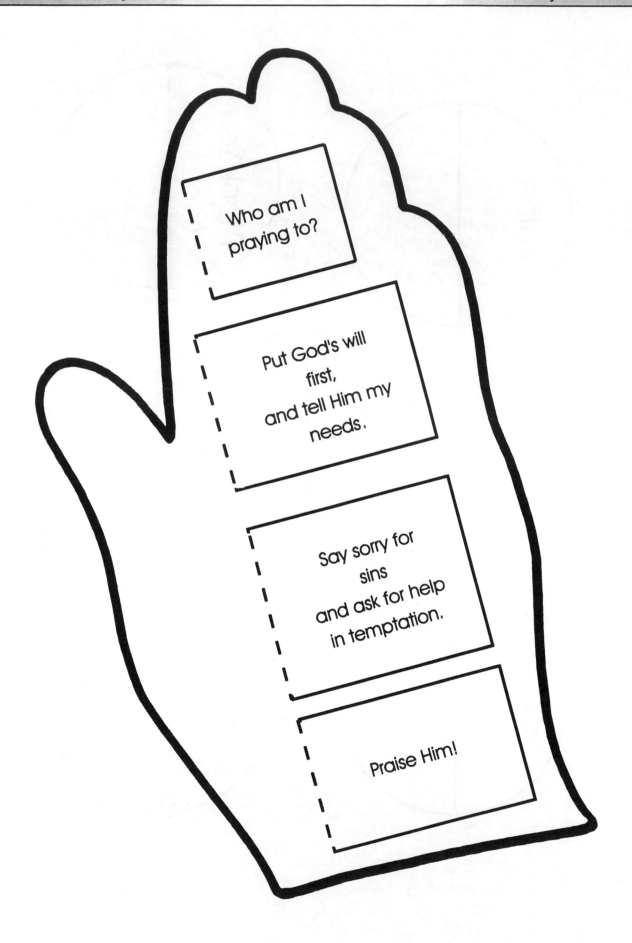

Who am I
praying to?

Put God's will
first,
and tell Him my
needs.

Say sorry for
sins
and ask for help
in temptation.

Praise Him!

Let us pray

Our Father
in heaven,
hallowed be
your name.

Your Kingdom come.
Your will be done on
earth as in heaven.
Give us today our
daily bread.

Forgive us our sins
as we forgive those
who sin against us.
Lead us not into
temptation, but deliver
us from evil.

For the kingdom,
the power and the
glory are yours,
now and forever,
Amen.

glue

glue

glue

glue

glue

Preparation:
Read Luke 18:1-8, using the Bible study notes to help you.

God and the judge are contrasted, not compared, e.g. the contrast between, 'For a while he refused' (the judge) and, 'Will he delay?' (of God). If even an unjust judge will grant justice to those who ask, how much more can we trust in the certainty and swiftness of God's answer.

A sign of the true disciple is that he will practise constant contact with God, who he knows will always hear his prayer. The answer may not always be what we hope; sometimes it is 'No', often 'Wait'. We learn that God answers speedily when we pray, and this encourages us to pray more often. We need, therefore, to persist in prayer believing it will bear much fruit. It is in this sense that the Son of Man, when he returns, will find faith within the Christian community at prayer.

Lesson Plan

Start by asking the children to tell you what they asked someone for yesterday. Who was the person, what was asked for, did they get it and, if not, why not? Do they have to keep on asking sometimes before getting an answer? Remind the children of last week's lesson on the Lord's Prayer. What things did Jesus tell his friends to ask God for? Does God always answer straight away? Jesus told people a story to teach them how to pray. (The older children should be told that the story was a parable - a story about a situation the hearers would recognise, which would cause them to think about what it meant to belong to God's kingdom.)

At the end of the story ask the children what sort of things they should pray about. Remind them of the

Lesson aim:
To teach the importance of persisting in prayer, being certain that God will answer.

importance of persisting in prayer. End with a time of prayer, encouraging the children to pray simple one sentence prayers.

Visual aids

Pictures of the woman and the judge. You might be able to find suitable pictures in a Child's Story Bible.

Activities / 3 - 5s

The children will make a model of the widow. Each child requires the following:
- pages 16 and 17 photocopied on card
- 1 toilet roll inner tube or ½ paper towel inner tube
- 2 pipe cleaners
- a dress and scarf cut from material
- a length of wool or a rubber band to be a belt.

Prior to the lesson cut out the shapes from pages 16 and 17 and put the hands, feet, face and hair into an envelope for each child. Do **not** cut the slits for the hair until it has been coloured. Cut out a dress and scarf for each child, using the templates on pages 16 and 17. Cut the centre slit on each dress where indicated. Add a dress and scarf to each envelope. Make 2 holes for the pipe cleaner arms in each cardboard tube, insert the pipe cleaners and make a loop for each hand. The arms must be long enough for the hands to meet in prayer.

Instructions
- Colour the face and glue it around the cardboard tube above the arms.
- Put the dress over the head and secure around the waist with a length of wool or a rubber band.
- Colour the hair, cut the slits and glue in place.
- Glue the front of the scarf to the head. Knot the ends loosely at chin level.
- Glue the card hands to the pipe cleaner loops, making sure that the thumbs are towards the face.
- Glue the feet to the back of the dress with the toes protruding slightly beyond the edge of the cardboard tube. Fold the feet back so that the woman is 'kneeling down'.

The teacher should make one at home as a model for the children to copy.

The children will make a perseverance cube. Photocopy page 18 on card and page 17 on paper for each child. Prior to the lesson cut out the cube from page 18, score and fold along dotted lines.

Instructions

- Glue the cube together. You may need some sellotape to ensure that it is firmly fixed.
- Colour the figures on page 17. The children draw their own hairstyle on the face above 'Thank you, God' and colour it appropriately.
- Cut out the 6 squares and glue them onto the cube in any order.
- The children throw or roll their cubes gently until they get the 'Thank you, God' side uppermost.

Point out to the children that they may often have to ask God several times before he answers their prayers, but sometimes God answers straight away. Do stress that praying to God is not a gamble, but we need to persevere, just as Jesus taught.

Each child requires pages 19 and 20 photocopied on paper and an A4 sheet of coloured paper. Prior to the lesson cut out the sections from page 19 by cutting along the thick black lines, and place in an envelope for each child.

Answer the questions on page 20 and colour the picture. Glue the cut out sections onto the coloured sheet of paper to make the original rectangle. Stress the need to keep persevering.

The Forgiving King   Activity for 7-9s

See page 67.

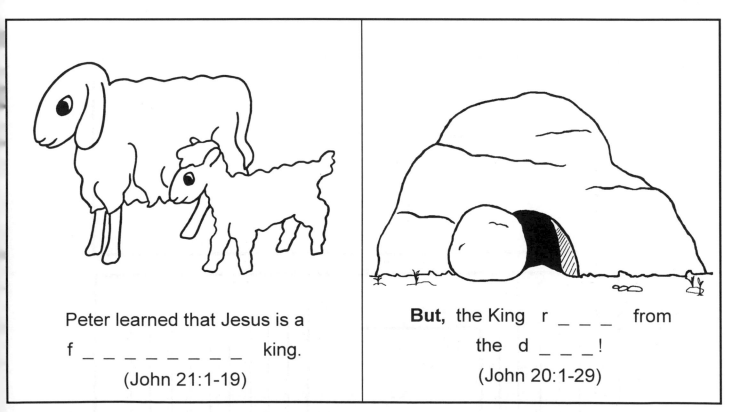

Peter learned that Jesus is a

f _ _ _ _ _ _ _ _ king.

(John 21:1-19)

But, the King r _ _ _ from

the d _ _ _!

(John 20:1-29)

robe template

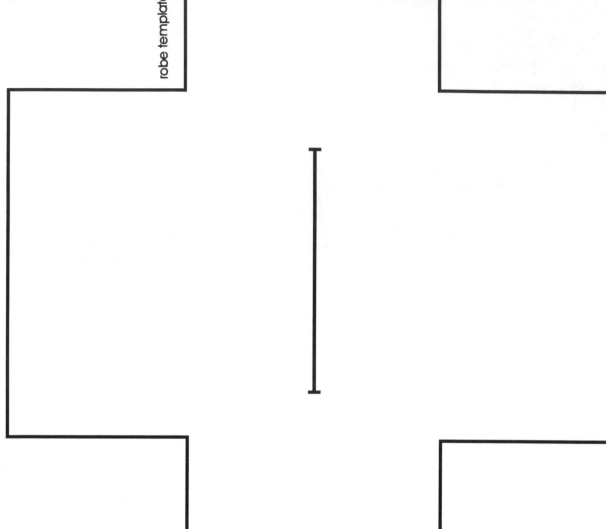

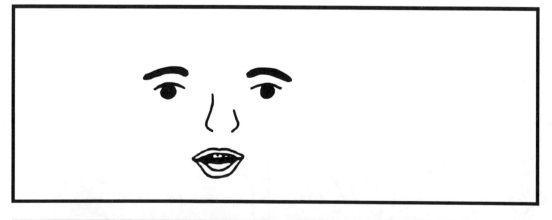

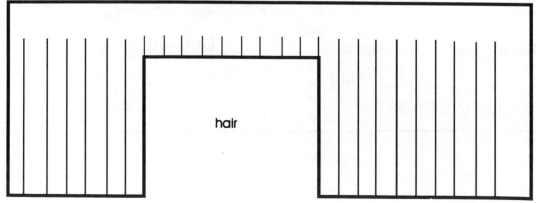

hair

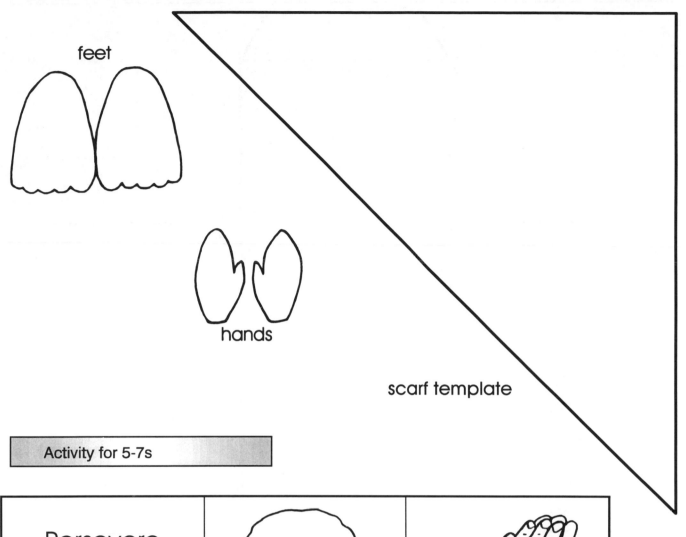

feet

hands

scarf template

Persevere
in
Prayer

Luke 18:1-8

Thank you, God.

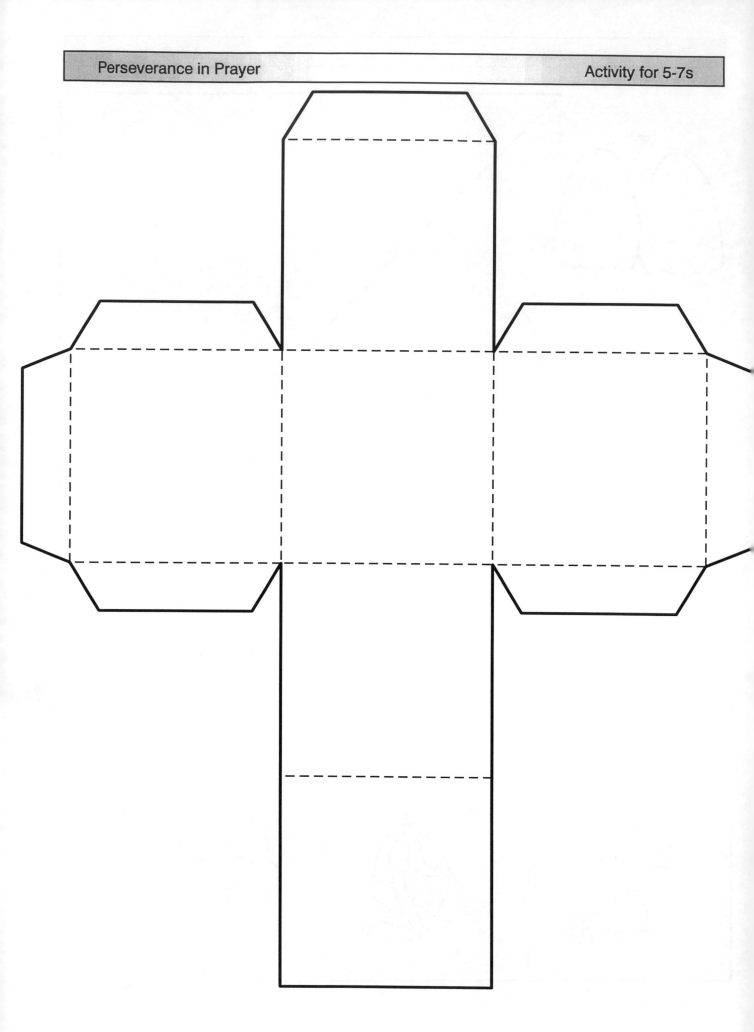

God answers prayers!

Persevere in Prayer

1. Did the widow give up when she got no help from the judge?

☐ yes   ☐ no

2. Did the judge help the widow because he was just?

☐ yes   ☐ no

3. Is God just?   ☐ yes   ☐ no

4. Should we give up if God does not appear to answer our prayers?

☐ yes   ☐ no

Preparation:
Read Luke 18:9-14, using the Bible study notes to help you.

Lesson aim:
To understand that we are able to draw near to God on the basis of what he has done for us, not what we have done for him.

In this parable Jesus contrasts the Pharisee with the tax-collector. The Pharisee was sure of his own righteousness and despised the tax-collector; the tax-collector knew he was a sinner and prayed for God to have mercy on him.

18:10   The Pharisees were a Jewish sect drawn mainly from the middle classes. At the time of Jesus they held a dominant position in the Sanhedrin (the Jewish ruling council). They were meticulous in keeping the Mosaic law and stressed the importance of tithing as a mark of loyalty to God.

      The tax-collectors were employed by the Romans to collect the taxes imposed on all subject peoples. They were often dishonest, keeping a portion of what they had collected for themselves (Luke 19:8). As a result, they were hated by the Jews. The Pharisees also despised tax collectors because their daily contact with their Gentile Roman masters made them ritually impure.

18:12   The Day of Atonement was the only fast required by law (Leviticus 16:29-34).
Leviticus 27:30-32 states the tithes required by law. These were required from all crops and livestock and were given to the Levites as a recognition of their service in the tabernacle/temple (Numbers 18:21-24). The Levites were then required to give a tithe of the tithe to the priests (Numbers 18:25-32). The Pharisees insisted that **all** food should be tithed, not just what came out of the ground. Therefore, the Pharisee in the parable was doing more than the law required.

18:14   The tax-collector, aware of his need for mercy, was the one whom God justified. The Pharisee, full of what he had done for God, had need of nothing - and got nothing!

It is easy for children to become complacent about their standing in God's sight, and to see praying, reading the Bible, going to church, etc. as signs of their own goodness. They need to be made aware that we do these things in obedience to God - not in order to win God's favour, but rather as a way of saying thank you for favour already bestowed (salvation). We come to God in prayer on the basis of what he has done for us, not what we have done for him.

Lesson Plan

Start by asking the children why God listens to their prayers. Pin up pictures of the sort of things that they might think make them acceptable to God, e.g. going to church, saying prayers, reading the Bible, giving money, Christian parents, being good (see the pictures on page 23). Ask the children to indicate which of these things cause God to listen to their prayers. In today's true story from the Bible we will see who is right.

At the end of the story go through the pictures again, ending with the picture of the cross. Talk about the tax-collector saying sorry to God. Discuss the sort of things we need to say sorry about. End with sorry prayers, encouraging the children to pray simple one sentence prayers.

Visual aids

Pictures of the Pharisee and the tax-collector, either full figures or just faces. The Pharisee needs to look satisfied; the tax-collector needs to look sad. (You might like to enlarge the figures on page 25.) If using faces only, have the mouth section attached with a split pin paper fastener so that it can be turned round. The tax-collector starts sad - but goes away happy (right in God's sight). The Pharisee is the opposite.

Activities / 3 - 5s

Make Pharisee and Tax-collector finger puppets. Photocopy this page for each child. Prior to the lesson cut out both bodies and arms and place in an envelope for each child.

- Colour both bodies and arm pieces. The arm pieces should be coloured on both sides.
- Roll the bodies into cylinders and glue along the dotted area.
- Glue the arms onto the body at the back.
- Use the puppets to act out the story.

Activities / 5 - 7s

Photocopy pages 23 and 24 for each child. Page 24 can be photocopied on coloured paper if desired. Prior to the lesson cut out the pictures and arrow and place in an envelope for each child. The children glue the pictures in the appropriate places on the base sheet. Attach the arrow to the base sheet at X, using a split pin paper fastener, so that the arrow can be moved to point at each picture in turn. Colour the pictures.

Activities / 7 - 9s

Photocopy pages 25 and 26 for each child. The children colour and cut out the figures on page 25, cutting along the thick black lines. Fold along the dotted line at the top of each figure. Glue the top flaps of 1 Pharisee and 1 tax-collector onto the boxes under each question on page 26 so that, when the figure is lifted up, the correct answer is visible underneath.

Finger Puppets for 3 - 5s

Pharisee

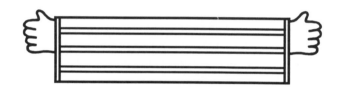

Tax-collector

Which one makes me right in God's sight?

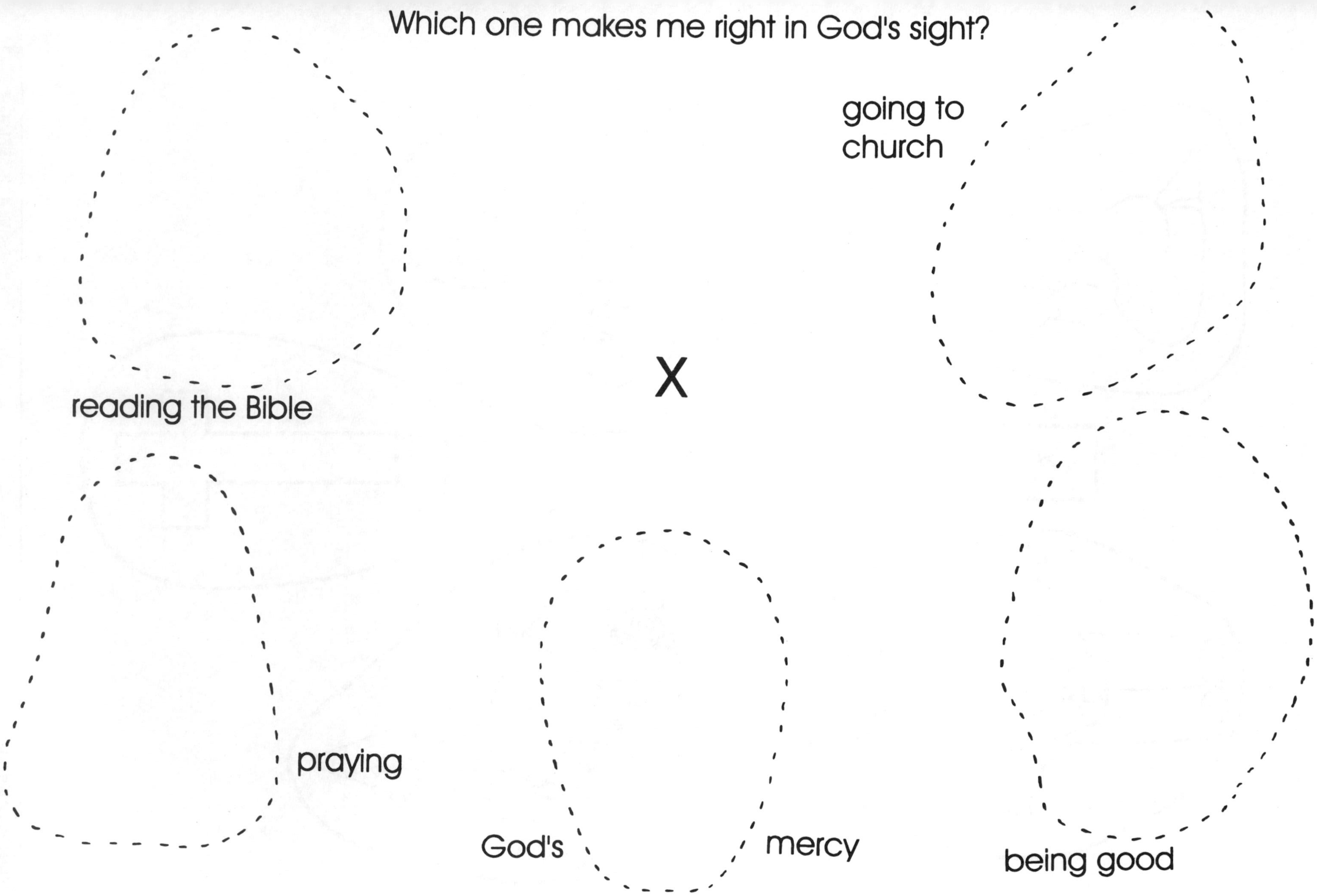

reading the Bible

going to
church

praying

X

God's
mercy

being good

The Parable of the Pharisee and the Tax-collector   (Luke 18:9-14)

Pharisees   Tax-collectors

Pharisees   Tax-collectors

The Pharisee and the Tax-collector Luke 18:9-14

Which one kept God's law?

[_____]   [_____]

yes   no

Which one thought he was right with God?

[_____]   [_____]

yes   no

Which one was right with God?

[_____]   [_____]

no   yes - he
                                              asked God
                                              for mercy

Preparation:
Read Matthew 18:19-35, using the Bible study notes to help you.

Lesson aim:
To show that God expects us to forgive others in the same way that he has forgiven us.

This parable follows on from a discourse on church discipline (18:15-17), and verses 18-20 must be read in the light of this. The Christian community has a duty to exercise discipline on its members, and should do so carefully and prayerfully. If done in this way and according to God's will it will have the authority of Christ. Peter then asks Jesus how often you have to forgive a Christian brother who sins against you, and Jesus answers with a parable that teaches about the extent of forgiveness. It is a fitting illustration of the petition about forgiveness in the Lord's prayer (Matthew 6:12,14-15).

18:21   The law allowed for equivalent revenge (Exodus 21:24), so Peter probably thought 7 times was being generous!!

18:22   The point of 70 X 7 (or 77) times is not that you can stop forgiving someone once the magic number has been reached; forgiveness is unlimited.

18:27   The king had a perfect right to sell the slave, his family and his possessions. The forgiveness offered was totally undeserved.

18:33   Being forgiven by God is the only true basis for human mercy.
Children find it quite easy to harbour a grudge against someone who has wronged them 'I hate him/her' is an often heard expression. If we cannot forgive others, we must question whether we are, in fact, forgiven by God.

Lesson Plan

Start by recapping on the previous 3 lessons. See if the children can remember why Jesus told stories (parables). What were the points of the parables they heard last week and the week before? Then ask the children if anyone has done anything horrid or hurt them during the last week. Talk about any situations that are volunteered. Did the person say sorry? Did the hurt person forgive him/her? Is it a good thing to forgive people? What about someone who keeps on doing wrong things - should we continue to forgive that person? Jesus told a story about how often we should forgive people.

At the end of the story point the children back to the Lord's Prayer, especially the petition on forgiveness. End with a time of prayer, encouraging the children to say simple sorry prayers. Finish with the Lord's prayer.

Visual aids

Pictures or flannelgraph. You might want to enlarge and colour the pictures on pages 29 and 30.

The parable can be acted out in class.

Activities / 3 - 5s

The children will make a book to tell the story. Photocopy pages 29, 30 and 31 for each child. Take page 31 and an A4 sheet of plain paper and fold them in half to make a book with the title on the front cover. Staple at the fold. Write on the bottom of the remaining pages as follows:

page 1 A servant owed a king millions of pounds, which he could not repay.

page 2 The king ordered the servant to be sold as a slave in order to repay the debt.

page 3 The servant asked the king to give him time to repay what he owed. The king forgave him the whole debt.

page 4 The servant went out and met another servant, who owed him a few pounds.

page 5 The servant sent his fellow servant to gaol, because he could not pay what he owed.

page 6 The king was very angry with the first servant, because he had not forgiven his fellow servant.

Prior to the lesson cut out the pictures from the remaining 2 pages and place in an envelope for each child. Go through the book with the children, asking them to find the appropriate picture for each page. Glue the pictures into the book and draw prison bars over the unforgiving servant on the back cover. Colour if time permits.

Activities / 5 - 7s

Photocopy page 32 single sided and pages 33 and 34 back to back for each child. Prior to the lesson cut out the 9 pictures from page 32 and place in an envelope for each child. The children sort out which picture goes with which text and glue the pictures in the appropriate spaces in the comic. There is no picture for the forgiven servant - the children draw a happy mouth on the face. After the 2 pictures of the servant in gaol have been glued in, the children draw prison bars over them. Colour the pictures if time permits.

Activities / 7 - 9s

Use the activity time to discuss the following situations.

1. Your best friend at school does not want to play with you and spends every play-time playing with someone else. The next day your friend comes up to you as though nothing has happened.
   Do you -
   - tell your friend to get lost - you are playing with someone else today?
   - play with your friend and with the other person?
   - play with your friend and exclude the other person?

2. You are playing football in the playground. A player on the other side kicks you on the leg. He says, 'Sorry!' - but you know he meant to kick you.
   Do you -
   - say, 'That's all right.' and carry on with the game?
   - shout at him and refuse to play with him again?
   - say, 'That's all right.' and make sure you get a chance to give him a kick later in the game?

3. You are playing a game at home in your bedroom. There are a lot of pieces on the floor, all set up in the right place. Your brother or sister comes barging in and breaks up the game. He/she says, 'Sorry!' - but the game is ruined.
   Do you -
   - throw something at your brother/sister and tell him/her to get out and never come into your room again?
   - go immediately into your brother or sister's bedroom and destroy a game he/she is playing?
   - accept the apology and ask your brother/sister to help you set up the game again?

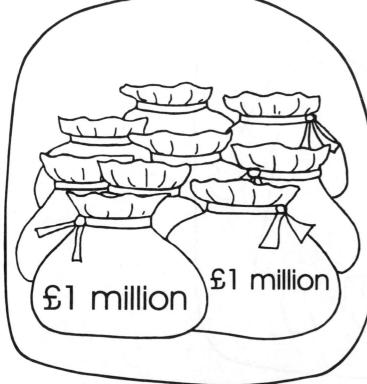

£1 million £1 million

The Story of
the
Unforgiving
Servant.

Matthew 18:19-35

The king sent the servant to gaol.

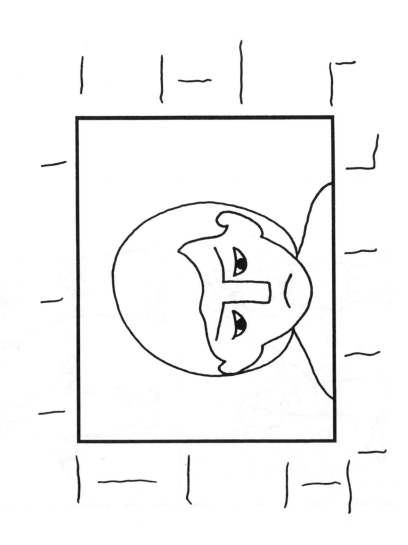

Forgive us our sins, as
we forgive those who
sin against us.
Matthew 6:12

The Story of

the

Unforgiving

Servant

Matthew 18:19-35

A servant owed a king millions of pounds, which he could not repay.

The king ordered the servant to be sold as a slave in order to repay the debt.

The servant asked the king for time to repay what he owed.

The king forgave the servant all his debt.

This servant went out and met another servant, who owed him a few pounds.

"Pay me what you owe!" he said.

The servant asked his fellow servant for time to pay what he owed.

But the servant would not listen. He sent his fellow servant to gaol.

The king was very angry with the first servant, because he had not forgiven his fellow servant.

The king sent the unforgiving servant to gaol.

Forgive us our sins,
as we forgive those
who sin against us.

Matthew 6:12

Jesus is King

Week 5	THE TRUSTED KING	*Matthew 14:22-33*
	To teach the need to trust God, whatever the circumstances.	
Week 6	THE SERVANT KING	*John 13:1-38*
	To teach that our love for God and one another is demonstrated by our service.	
Week 7	THE BETRAYED KING	*Matthew 26:31-58,69-75*
	To teach the need to watch and pray if we are not to fall into temptation.	
Good Friday	THE REJECTED KING	*John 18:28 - 19:42*
	To teach that Jesus' death on the cross was according to God's plan.	
Week 8	THE RISEN KING	*John 20:1-29*
	To teach that Jesus' resurrection is our only source of hope.	
Week 9	THE FORGIVING KING	*John 21:1-19*
	To teach that God is willing to use anyone who truly repents of their sin.	

Series Aims

1. To understand the stories in their context.

2. To understand the need for total trust in and dependence on God if we are to serve him faithfully.

This series looks at Jesus as King and our relationship with him. Apart from the Good Friday lesson, the passages studied deal with Peter's relationship with Jesus. The lesson for Good Friday looks at the rejection of Jesus by Jew and Gentile and comes after Peter's denial of Jesus and before the hope generated by the empty tomb. Peter was the first disciple to confess that Jesus is the Christ, the Son of the living God (Matthew 16:15-16), but Peter's view of what that meant was very different from God's (Matthew 16:21-28).

The first lesson of the series deals with Peter walking on the water to Jesus and our need to trust Jesus whatever our circumstances. The second lesson is the story of Jesus washing his disciples' feet and looks at how we serve God and one another. The third lesson carries on from the previous one, dealing with Jesus in the Garden of Gethsemene and Peter's denial of Jesus. In the Easter Sunday lesson (week 8) we study Jesus' resurrection and the series ends with a lesson on Jesus challenging Peter regarding Peter's love for him.

The aim of this series is to teach the children the biblical view of Jesus' kingship and to help them understand their need to trust him if they are to serve him faithfully.

Memory Work

3-5s   Trust in the Lord with all your heart.
Proverbs 3:5

5-9s   Trust in the Lord with all your heart. Never rely on what you think you know.
Proverbs 3:5

Preparation:
Read Matthew 14:22-33, using the Bible study notes to help you.

Lesson aim:
To teach the need to trust God, whatever the circumstances.

Lesson Plan

This incident occurs immediately after the feeding of the 5,000.

14:22   It is not certain which part of Lake Galilee was being crossed. According to Luke, the feeding of the 5,000 took place in the region of Bethsaida (Luke 9:10-12). Mark implies that the boat was on its way to Bethsaida (Mark 6:45), whereas John states that it was crossing towards Capernaum (John 6:17).

14:24   The boat was approximately 3-3½ miles from land (John 6:19).

14:25   The fourth watch was between 3 and 6 a.m.

14:28   This was typical of Peter's impetuosity!

14:30   Peter had committed himself to a course of action without considering the difficulties. Once he started to look at the difficulties, he sank.

14:33   Remind the children of the reason for miracles to cause people to believe in Jesus (John 20:30-31).

This is the first lesson of a new series, so spend some time introducing it. Prior to the lesson make a list of pairs of friends that the children will know, e.g. Tom & Jerry, Yogi Bear & Booboo, Popeye & Olive Oil, Bert & Ernie (Sesame Street), Zig & Zag, etc. Write each name on a piece of card. Muddle up the cards and place on a table or board. Ask the children to put the pairs together. Once the exercise has been completed discuss what it is that makes friends special. What if your special friend is a king? Over the next 5 weeks we will find out about Peter and his special friendship with Jesus.

At the end of the story review what Peter has learnt about Jesus and teach the memory verse.

Visual aids

Use flannelgraph or big pictures with moving pieces. Peter has to 'walk' across the water and 'sink' behind the waves. Figures required are Peter, the group of disciples, a boat. The activity for 5-7s on pages 39 and 40 could be enlarged, coloured and used.

Activities / 3 - 5s

Photocopy page 38 on paper and the big figure of Peter with tab from page 39 on card for each child. Prior to the lesson cut out the figure of Peter and cut a slit where indicated on page 38. The children colour the figure of Peter and the picture. Insert Peter through the slit so that he is walking on the sea. Gradually pull the tab down to show what happened when Peter stopped trusting Jesus.

Activities / 5 - 7s

Each child requires page 40 photocopied on paper, the boat and small figure of Peter from page 39 photocopied on card and one A4 sheet of blue paper. Prior to the lesson cut out the figures from page 39 plus 1 strip approximately 1.5 cm wide from the bottom of the page. Cut the sheet of blue paper in half lengthways then cut off the excess to leave 2 strips 9 cm wide. Cut the tops to make waves (see diagram). Cut the slot in page 40 where indicated.

Instructions

- Glue one wave strip to page 40 with the bottom along the dotted line. From the back of the page recut the slot through the blue wave strip.

- Glue or staple the figure of Peter onto the strip of card with the strip projecting horizontally from the back of the feet. Insert the strip through the slot on page 40 so that Peter is walking from the right of the picture.

- Glue the boat to the back of the second wave strip at the right hand side (see diagram).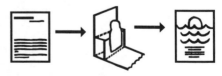

- Glue the second wave strip onto the picture with the base at the bottom of the picture. NB Only glue along the bottom and sides of this wave strip. If the figure of Peter is placed as far to the right of the picture as possible he will appear to be in the boat. Move Peter out of the boat and towards the left of the picture (towards Jesus). As Peter gets further from the boat he can be made to sink by moving his strip upwards.

- Colour if time permits.

Activities / 7 - 9s

Photocopy page 41 for each child.

- Cut the page in half lengthways along the solid line.

- Fold side A in half along dotted line so that the text is on the outside.

- On side B cut around the top part of Peter's body along the thick black line from the lower dotted line on either side.
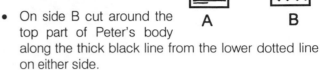

- Fold side B as follows:
  - fold the picture sides together along the dotted line beneath Peter's feet,
  - fold the plain sides together along the lower dotted line either side of Peter's body,
  - fold the picture sides together along the upper dotted line either side of Peter's body.
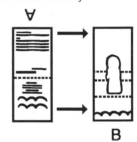

- Glue sides A and B together, starting at the bottom. Only glue from the lower fold on side B down and the upper fold on side B up.

- Fold in half along the fold on side A, ensuring that Peter stays upright within the card.

- Trim off any overlap along the top of the card. Cut along the wavy line on the bottom of the card to make waves.

- Start with the story on the front of the card, then open up to show Peter walking on the water to Jesus. Bring the bottom of the card up to show what happened to Peter when he stopped trusting Jesus.
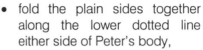

- Colour if time and draw in a wavy sea above the text on the front.

Trust in the Lord with all your heart.

Proverbs 3:5

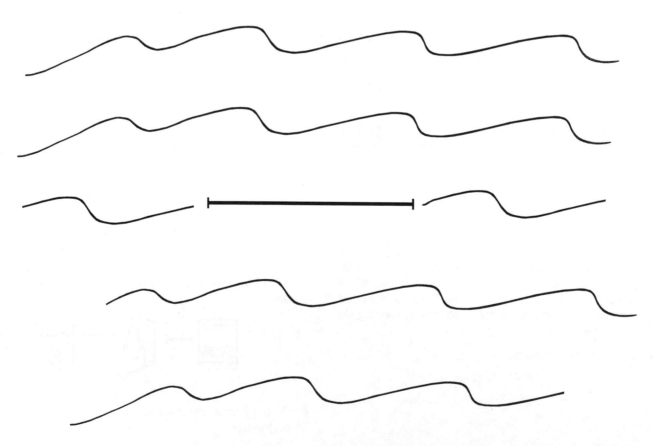

Peter did not trust Jesus when he saw the strong wind and big waves. He began to sink!

Tab ↓

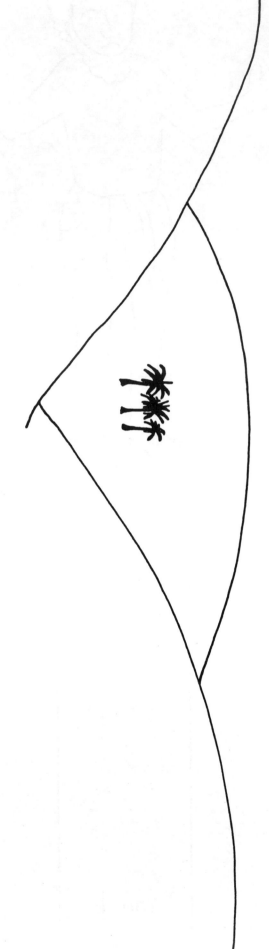

Trust in the Lord with all your heart.   Proverbs 3:5

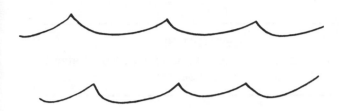

Trust in the Lord with
all your heart.
Never rely on what
you think you know.

Proverbs 3:5

The Trusted King

Matthew 14:22-33

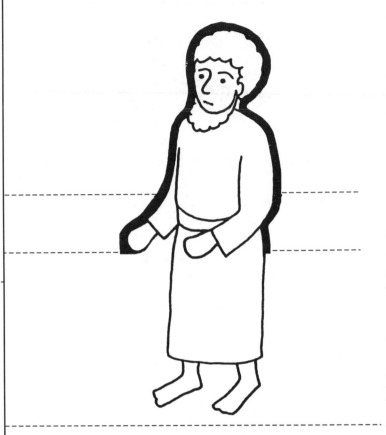

Peter and the other disciples were in a boat. It was night time, the wind was blowing and the waves were rough. Jesus walked across the surface of the lake toward the boat.

Peter said: "If it is really you, Lord, tell me to come to you."

Jesus said: "Come."

Peter got out of the boat and walked towards Jesus. But when Peter saw the wind and the waves he was afraid and began to sink.

Peter cried: "Lord, save me!"

Immediately Jesus reached out his hand and caught him. Then they both climbed into the boat.

Preparation:
Read John 13:1-38, using the Bible study notes to help you.

Lesson aim:
To teach that our love for God is demonstrated by our service.

See also Matthew 26:17-30, Mark 14:12-31, Luke 22:7-38.

13:1   This verse sets the scene, bringing out the importance of what was to follow - the symbolic act of foot washing.

13:4-5   A slave would have worn a loin cloth and wrapped a long strip of material around his waist, using the end as a towel. Foot washing was the job of a slave, not the job of the Teacher (Rabbi).

13:7   Jesus is referring to the time after the resurrection when he talks about 'later'.

13:8   Note Peter calls Jesus 'Lord' in v.6, then does not want to do what Jesus says. Peter does not want Jesus to demean himself by doing the job of a servant.

13:9   Note Peter's reversal of attitude and its extravagance - 'Wash all of me'.

13:10   Once we belong to Jesus we are clean in God's sight - but our sins still need to be dealt with on a daily basis.

13:11   John underlines Jesus' knowledge that Judas would betray him.

13:12-17   Jesus was calling his followers to behave in a way which would have been despised by the world as weakness. The children need to understand that following Jesus will sometimes result in them being laughed at by their peers.

13:18   See Psalm 41:9.

13:23   'The disciple whom Jesus loved' was John.

13:31   'Son of Man' would have been recognised as a reference to the Messiah - see Daniel 7:13-14.

13:34   The commands to love God, and to love my neighbour were not new (Deuteronomy 6:5, Leviticus 19:18, Luke 10:27). What was new was the motivation - to love one another in the way that Jesus loves us.

Lesson Plan

Discuss with the children what happens when they go to a party or to a friend's house for tea. Do they wash their hands before they sit down to eat? Explain that the country Jesus and his friends lived in was a hot country. People wore sandals and walked everywhere, so their feet became very dirty. When people sat down for a meal one of the servants washed their feet before they ate. Tell the story.

At the end of the story discuss with the children how they can show that they love Jesus. Revise the memory verse.

Act out the story as you tell it with the teacher being Jesus and children being disciples. You will need a bowl of water and a towel, bread and blackcurrant juice (or similar). **NB** Whoever is 'sent out' as Judas needs to be brought back in to hear the rest of the lesson!

Activities / 3 - 5s

Photocopy page 44 for each child. Prior to the lesson cut off the strip at the end of the page and cut out the circle. Cut out the marked section on the picture. The children colour the picture and the smaller segment of the circle to represent water. Attach the circle behind the picture at X using a split pin paper fastener. Rotate the circle to show water flowing from the jug into the bowl.

Activities / 5 - 7s

Photocopy pages 43, 45 and the top half of page 51 for each child. Prior to the lesson cut out the 6 pictures from pages 43 and 51 and place in an envelope for each child. The children glue the picture showing what Jesus did into the top frame on page 45. Choose 5 pictures showing service and glue into 5 of the frames. Draw or write a further illustration of service in the blank frame. Colour the pictures if time permits.

Activities / 7 - 9s

Photocopy page 46 for each child. Do the puzzle as a group activity so that the less able do not get left behind. You might want to pin up an enlarged version on a board or flip chart to show the way through the maze. Write the letters into the blank spaces below as you come to them. This will help the children sort out where one word ends and the next begins.

Discuss with the children how they can serve each other. Point out the dangers of relying on what they think they know (like Peter), rather than on God's word.

Bringing Mummy and Daddy a cup of tea.

Reading a Christian book.

Sharing

Playing with friends.

Knowing all the books of the Bible.

Playing with a new boy or girl.

Being good in class.

Trust in the Lord with all your heart.

Proverbs 3:5

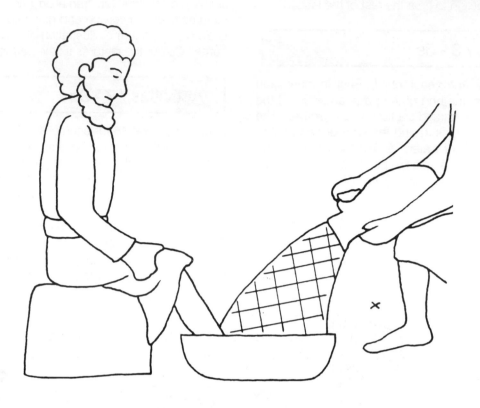

Jesus showed his friends how much he loved them by washing their feet.

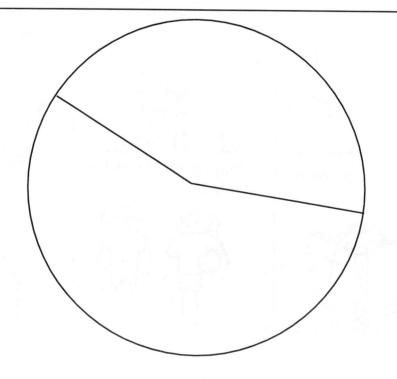

Pictures of Service

Jesus did this to teach his disciples about service.

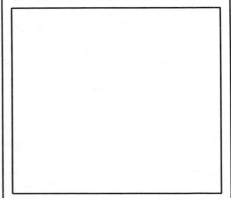

We can serve by doing these things.

Trace your memory verse through both feet to discover something that Peter needed to learn. On each foot start at the arrow and end at the star, putting in arrows as you go. As you come to them write the letters in the dashed spaces below.

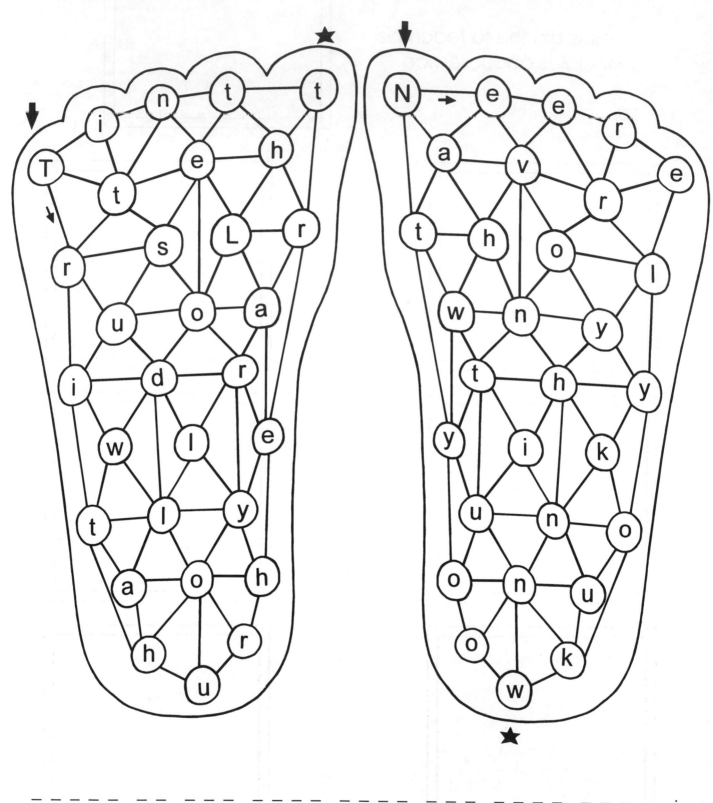

_ _ _ _ _   _ _ _ _   _ _ _ _   _ _ _ _   _ _ _ _ _   _ _ _ _ _ _ .

_ _ _ _ _   _ _ _ _ _ _   _ _ _ _   _ _ _ _ _   _ _ _ _ _ _ .

Proverbs 3:5

46

WEEK 7
The Betrayed King

Preparation:
Read Matthew 26:31-58,69-75, using the Bible study notes to help you.

Lesson aim:
To teach the need to watch and pray if we are not to fall into temptation.

26:31 See Zechariah 13:7. Note the change of tense from 'strike' to 'I will strike'. Perhaps Jesus is signifying that God is in control of events.

26:33 Demonstrates Peter's impetuosity.

26:35 Peter is unwilling to accept Jesus' view of the situation (v.34). See Jeremiah 17:9 and 1 Corinthians 10:11-13.

26:39 The cup is the cup of suffering (see 26:27-28; 20:22, Isaiah 51:22).

26:40 Peter, having recently stated that he would never forsake Jesus, cannot even keep awake when Jesus asks him (v.38).

26:51 cf. John 18:10.

26:58 Peter follows at a distance. He is allowed to enter the courtyard because he is with John, who is known to the High Priest (John 18:15-16).

26:70-74 Note how Peter's denials increase in vehemence. Peter was afraid. It would be worth discussing our behaviour when we are afraid with the children (especially with the older ones). What situations make them afraid and how do they react in these situations (e.g. lying to get out of trouble)?

Also discuss what they can do to overcome their fear and the importance of not denying Jesus, either by words or actions (or just by keeping silent). See Mark 8:38.

26:75 Peter's remorse was genuine. Discuss with the children how Peter may have felt at that moment.

Lesson Plan

Ask the children if they are ever afraid. What do they do when they are afraid? Probably they will talk about being afraid of such things as spiders and going to a parent for comfort. Lead the conversation round to what happens when they have done something naughty and have been found out. Do they always own up? If not, why not? Today's true story from the Bible is about someone who was afraid. Ask the children if they can remember which of Jesus' friends they have been learning about. Recap on the last 2 lessons, using a question and answer format. Tell the story.

At the end of the story talk about how Peter may have felt, how he was truly sorry. Refer back to the previous series on prayer. What should we do when we do naughty things? Revise the memory verse. Finish with a short time of prayer, encouraging the children to pray simple sorry prayers.

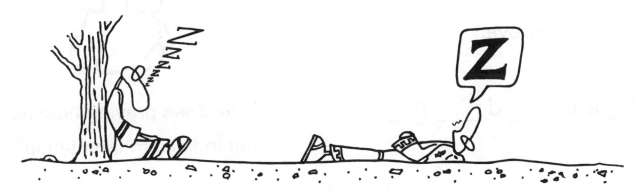

Pictures or flannelgraph. You only need pictures of the main characters. It might be appropriate to use pictures from a Child's Story Bible. If there is time the story can be acted out at the end of the lesson.

Activities / 3 - 5s

Make a story box. Photocopy page 49 on paper and page 50 on card for each child. Prior to the lesson make up the story box according to the instructions on page 50. Cut out the 4 pictures and place in an envelope for each child. The children colour the pictures then glue them around the box in the order of the story. Use the box to revise the story.

Activities / 5 - 7s

Photocopy pages 48/51 and 52/53 back to back for each child. Prior to the lesson cut both pages in half along the solid line. Take the 3 half pages and place together with 'Watch and Pray' on top, 'Jesus told his disciples to w_ _ _ _ and p_ _ _' in the middle, and 'Pray How does praying help us not to fall into temptation?' on the bottom. Fold the pages in half to make a booklet. Check that you have the order right before stapling at the fold. Go through the booklet as a class rather than individually.

Activities / 7 - 9s

Photocopy page 54 on card for each child and follow the instructions on the page.

When Mummy asks me to do something, but I want to do something else, I am often tempted to be

s _ _ f _ _ h

or even

d _ s o _ _ d _ _ n _ .

How does praying help us not to fall into temptation?

Jesus asked Peter, James and John to stay awake while he prayed.

They fell asleep

Soldiers arrested Jesus. They took him to the High Priest. Peter followed.

Peter was asked 3 times if he knew Jesus. Each time Peter said, 'No!'

side 4

1. Cut out, score and fold along dotted lines.
2. Glue side 4 to the remaining 3 sides.
3. Glue the top flaps inside the sides to make a box open at the bottom.

Trust in the Lord with all your heart.
Proverbs 3:5

Cheering up someone who is ill.

Washing up

The Betrayed King - activity for 5-7s

When my friends are doing wrong, I am sometimes tempted to join in because I don't want to be the odd one out.

God will know.

Come on, Lucy, no one will know.

KEEP OUT

I am sometimes tempted to

t _ _ l   l _ _ s.

How can watching and praying help?

This book belongs to

....

....

Jesus said:

Watch and pray so that you will not fall into temptation.

Matthew 26:41

Watch

How does watching help us not to fall into temptation?

How can watching and praying help?

Watch and Pray

How else am I tempted?

Jesus told
his disciples
to
w _ _ _ _
and
p _ _ _ .

How can watching and
praying help?

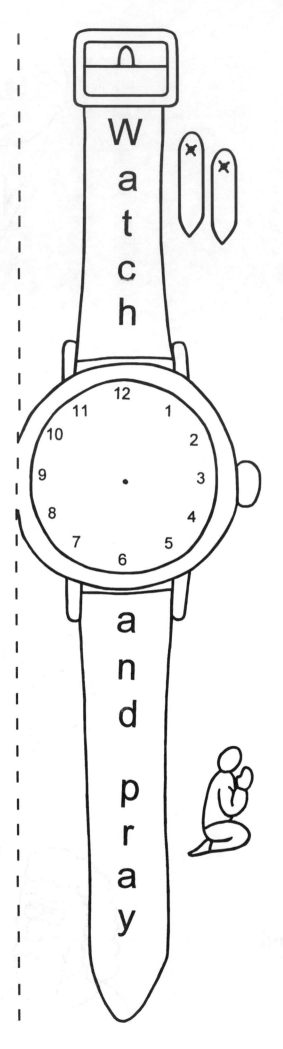

Bookmark or wall-hanging

1. Fold the page along the dotted line and, with page folded, cut out the watch shape.

2. Open up the shape and cut along the solid line between watch and both straps on the top shape only. Cut off the knob from the side of the bottom watch shape.

3. Glue the 2 cut off watch straps onto the straps on the bottom watch shape. You should have a watch with a face that can be opened.

4. Cut out the praying figure and glue inside the watch face so that it is visible when the watch is opened. Write the Bible reference for the memory verse underneath the praying figure.

5. If making a wall-hanging cut out the 2 watch hands, make holes at X and attach to the top watch face with a split pin paper fastener. Make sure the hands rotate freely. Make a hole at the buckle and attach a hanging loop of wool.

6. If making a bookmark draw on the watch hands.

7. Colour if time permits.

Preparation:
Read John 18:28 - 19:42, using the Bible study notes to help you.

Lesson aim:
To teach that Jesus' death on the cross was according to God's plan.

18:28   Note the Jewish authorities' desire to avoid ritual uncleanness! Cf. Jesus' teaching in Matthew 15:10-20 on what makes a person unclean. The authorities were only concerned with the externals; they were already unclean because of their plotting to kill Jesus.

18:31   Any death sentence passed by the Sanhedrin (Jewish Council) had to be ratified by the Roman Governor before being carried out.

18:32   The Roman form of execution for criminals was crucifixion. Note John's underlining of the fact that this happened to fulfil God's plan. Cf. John 13:11, Mark 8:31-38, John 3:14; 12:32-33.

18:36   Spiritual kingship is not demonstrated by the use of worldly power.

18:38-39   Pilate could find no reason to condemn Jesus, but was too weak to release him unconditionally. He still sought to curry favour with the Jews.

18:40   The people preferred a terrorist to Jesus!

19:1-4   Pilate was prepared to authorise punishment, even when he had no reason to believe a crime had been committed.

19:5   'Here is the man!' Pilate's statement meant more than he realised - on the cross Jesus took the place of man and took God's punishment for sin on himself.

19:7   The charge of blasphemy is introduced for the first time. Was this because the crowd thought Pilate was going to release Jesus and wanted to push him into passing the death sentence? The Romans had committed themselves to the maintenance of Jewish customs and law, so Pilate was now being asked to uphold the law.

19:11   Cf. Romans 13:1. The one who handed Jesus over to Pilate was Caiaphas, the High Priest.

19:12   'You are not Caesar's friend' - the final accusation that pushed Pilate into passing the death sentence.
Note the stages Pilate went through - wanting to please the Jews (18:38), wanting to keep the law (19:7-8), wanting to please his masters (19:12). This was sufficient to make him do what he knew to be unjustified.

19:15   Israel was a theocracy (governed by God as their king), so this statement by the chief priests was a denial of God.

19:17   The criminal carried his own crossbar to the place of execution. The main pole was already there.

19:22   A demonstration of Pilate's obstinacy.

19:23-24   Cf. Psalm 22:18.

19:28   Cf. Psalms 22:14-15; 69:21.

19:30   Note that Jesus gave up his life - he did not just die. The following verses demonstrate that the victims were not expected to die so soon, but death had to be hastened in order that the Passover might be celebrated without hindrance.

19:34   This demonstrated that Jesus really died and was not just unconscious.

19:35   'The man' probably refers to John. (See 13:23; 18:15; 19:26; 20:2-8; 21:21 for other times when John refers to himself in the 3rd person.)

19:36   Psalm 34:20, Exodus 12:43-46.

19:37   Zechariah 12:10.

19:38   Joseph of Arimathea was a member of the Sanhedrin (Luke 23:50-51).

19:39   See John 3:1-2. The amount of spices taken by Nicodemus would have cost a lot of money, so was evidence of Nicodemus' devotion to Jesus.

19:41   The new tomb meant that Jesus' body would not come into contact with decay - see Psalm 16:10.

Lesson Plan

As there will be fewer children (and helpers!) this lesson is better taught as one large group. In order to help the children understand that we are unable to save ourselves the following scenario is suggested. You need a helper (either a teacher or a puppet), a tray containing half a hot cross bun, a small box or bar of chocolate, a large box or bar of chocolate and an area to be the prison. Prior to the lesson hide the small box/bar of chocolate.

Tell the children that the helper has been busy preparing hot cross buns for them. Send an older child to get the tray of hot cross buns. When the child returns with the tray with half a hot cross bun ask the helper what has happened to them. Eventually the helper admits to eating them all. The helper is given a punishment - either provide a box (or bar) of chocolate as recompense or go to prison. The helper has no chocolate so is sent to prison. One of the other teachers suggests that the children might be able to help the one in prison by finding some chocolate. The children search for the chocolate. When it is found it is given to the leader, who says that it is not big enough. The helper must remain in prison.

Tell the story. During the story a teacher hides the large box/bar of chocolate. Either at the end or between the 2 sections of the story send the children off to find a bigger box/bar of chocolate to get the helper out of prison. When the children find the big chocolate it is offered to the leader to get the helper out of prison - but it is not big enough.

At the end of the session there is only one way to set the prisoner free - the leader takes the helper's place. One of the other teachers points out that Jesus took our place when he died on the cross and finishes with prayer.

Visual aids

Designate 2 areas of the room for the story - Pilate's courtyard and the crucifixion. If you have a flannelgraph you can set up the appropriate background in each area. If not, place a chair in Pilate's courtyard to be a throne. For the crucifixion make a simple background of a green hill. You also need 3 brown crosses to stick on the hill.

Prior to the story, divide the children into Jews and Gentiles. Divide the Jews into Caiaphas and Annas (High Priests), the crowd and the disciples. Divide the Gentiles into Pilate and Roman soldiers. Sit 'Pilate' on the chair for that part of the story. (You might want to be Pilate.) During the story the children can shout out for Barabbas and 'Crucify him'. Go in procession from the courtyard to the place of crucifixion.

At the end of the story, all the children stand up. Go through the events, starting with the arrest of Jesus. As each group rejects Jesus, (e.g. the disciples run away), the children in that group sit down. At the end no-one is left standing. Point out to the children that everyone rejected Jesus, (friends, Jews, Gentiles), and we would have done the same.

Activities / 3 - 9s

The activity is the same for each age group. Photocopy pages 58 and 59 back to back and page 57 single-sided for each child. Fold the double-sided page in half to make a booklet and cut out the 3 rectangles from page 57.

The activity is designed to teach the children about the substitutionary aspect of Jesus' death. This needs to be explained to the children, starting with Jesus dying in place of Barabbas, then reminding them of the following -
- Abraham being told to sacrifice Isaac and the provision of a ram,
- the death of the first born in Egypt and the provision of a lamb.

Continue by pointing out that the result of sin is death, we are all sinners, and Jesus died on the cross in my place, to take my punishment.

You will need pictures of these incidents. (These can be taken from pages 57, 58 and 59.)

The children go through the booklet, filling in the missing letters (younger children will need this doing for them) and gluing the edge of the appropriate picture against the line on the booklet so that the substitutionary object covers the underlying picture. All the rectangles should be folded along the dotted lines so that they will fold back to reveal the underlying picture.

lamb

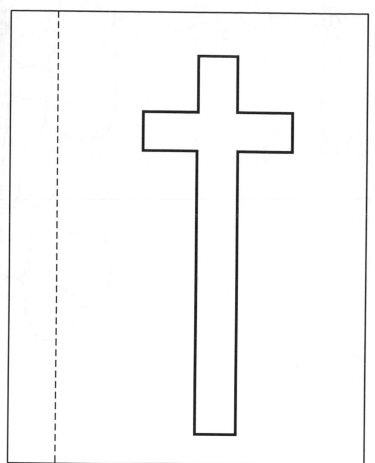

cross

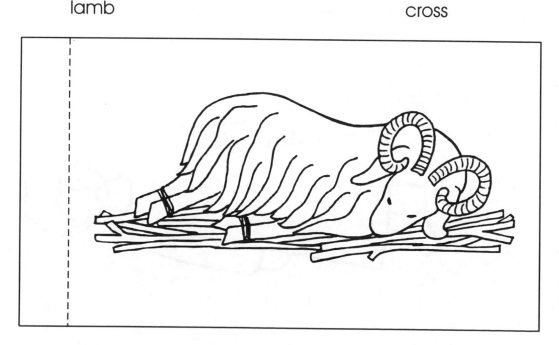

ram

ar _ _

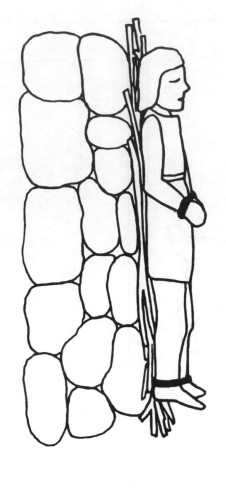

instead of Isaac,
Genesis 22:12-14

al _ _
_ _

instead of the first born,
Exodus 12:3-7, 12-13

God
provided ...

J _ _ _ _

instead of me.
John 11:49-52

Preparation:
Read John 20:1-29, using the Bible study notes to help you.

Lesson aim:
To teach that Jesus' resurrection is our only source of hope.

20:1   See Matthew 28:1, Mark 16:1-2, Luke 24:1. The tomb had been officially sealed - Matthew 27:57-66.

20:2   The disciple whom Jesus loved was John.

20:6   Peter is still the first of the disciples to do anything, - cf. walking on the water (Matthew 14:28-29), asserting that Jesus is the Messiah (Matthew 16:15-16), denying Jesus (Matthew 26:69-75).

20:7   This verse implies that the grave clothes were left in the position they would have been round the body, rather than in a jumbled heap (as would have happened if someone had pulled them off the body prior to removing it from the tomb).

20:9   See Psalm 16:10.

20:23   This does not imply that men can forgive sins - only God can do this (Mark 2:6-7). Men are able to reassure penitent people that their sins have been forgiven because of Christ's death on the cross. If people refuse to repent their sins will remain unforgiven.

Lesson Plan

Place a box of chocolates or large tube of mini Easter eggs on the table, having emptied and resealed it prior to the lesson. Ask a child to open it and hand the contents round. Once it has been discovered that it contains nothing, ask the children what has happened to the contents. They will tell you that someone has removed them. Ask the children if the contents could have removed themselves. Why not? Tell the story, including brief details of the crucifixion if that lesson has not been used.

At the end of the story go over the things that Peter has been learning about Jesus. Who is Jesus? Stress the fact that Jesus' resurrection proves that he is God and is able to look after us for ever.

Visual aids

Pictures or a model. Even though it comes round year after year the younger children enjoy a model of the Easter garden. Use a margarine container (or similar) for the tomb (see page 65). Either use peg people for the people in the story or the figures on page 65.

Peg People
Requirements
Wooden clothes pegs, scraps of material, pink or white paper, card, bluetak, pipe cleaners, cotton wool, needle and thread, glue, pens.

Instructions
- Wind a piece of paper around the top of the clothes peg and draw on a face.
- Wrap a pipe cleaner around the peg just below the face and make a loop at each end for the hands.
- Cut out a length of material twice the length of the peg and approximately 5 cm wide. Make a slit at the centre big enough to go over the top of the peg. Place the material over the top of the peg (see diagram).
- Wrap the material round the peg and use ½ a pipe cleaner as a belt.
- Make card feet (see diagram) and attach to the base of the peg with bluetak.
- Take a square of material approximately 6 x 6 cm to make the head-dress. For a man, attach the head-dress using ½ a pipe cleaner as a head band. For a woman, turn in the top edge of the material then wrap it round the face, securing it with a stitch.

The story can also be told using finger puppets (see instructions on page 22).

Activities / 3 - 5s

Photocopy page 62 single sided and pages 63 and 64 back to back for each child. Prior to the lesson cut along the solid lines on page 64 and fold back along the dotted lines.
The children colour the cross on page 63 and the picture on page 62. Glue page 63 on top of page 62, only gluing around the edges. The 4 sections of the cross can be opened to show the grave containing our sins at the base of the cross underneath. Explain that we can only be God's friends because Jesus died on the cross to take the punishment for all the naughty things we do.

Activities / 5 - 7s

Each child requires page 65 photocopied on card, 1 500 gm margarine tub, 1 A4 sheet of green card (optional), white tissues or scraps of material, and 5 strips of card measuring 6 x 1 cm.
- Cut out a piece of the margarine tub to make an opening. (This should be done in advance.)
- Cut out the stone and glue it to one side of the opening.
- Cut out the Bible verse and glue it round the outside of the container.
- Glue the margarine tub to the green card to make a base (optional).
- Cut out the 5 figures and glue on strips of card so that they will stand up.
- Put white 'grave clothes' in the tomb.
- Use the figures to act out the story.

Activities / 7 - 9s

The children will make a wall hanging depicting the empty tomb with the sun rising behind it.
Each child requires
- 1 A4 sheet of blue paper for the background
- some green paper to cut out a strip of grass
- some grey paper to cut out the rock tomb and stone
- some yellow paper to cut out the sun and its rays
- an envelope containing the letters to make the sentence 'Jesus is alive!' (These can be all one colour or a mix of colours.)
- a garden stick and a length of wool to make a hanging loop.

Instructions
- Glue the short side of the blue paper to the garden stick with the stick protruding at each end. This will be the top of the picture.
- From the grey paper cut out a rock tomb and stone.
- Cut out a sun from yellow paper.
- Position the tomb on the blue background with the sun rising from behind. Make sure there is sufficient space above it for the words 'Jesus is alive!' Glue sun and tomb in place.
- Using a black felt tip pen draw in an opening for the tomb.
- Cut out a strip of grass from green paper and glue in place under the tomb.
- Glue the stone to one side of the entrance.
- Cut out sun's rays from yellow paper and glue around the visible portion of the sun.
- Glue on the words 'Jesus is alive!'

• Attach the length of wool to each end of the garden stick to make a hanging loop.

If Jesus was still dead today ....

.... we would have no hope.

Trust in the Lord...

With all your heart,
Proverbs 3:5

God made Jesus alive again...

...so we can rejoice.

Mary Magdalene   John   angel

Simon Peter   angel

Trust in the Lord with all your heart. Never rely on what you think you know.   Proverbs 3:5

Preparation:
Read John 21:1-19, using the Bible study notes to help you.

Lesson aim:
To teach that God is willing to use anyone who truly repents of their sin.

21:1	The sea of Tiberias is the Sea of Galilee.
21:3	The one thing Peter knew he could do was fish - but they caught nothing. Peter could not even do the thing he was good at!
21:7	John realises who Jesus is before Peter does (cf. John 20:8).
21:8	Peter is still the same impetuous Peter.
21:9	There is already fish cooking over the fire. Jesus had no need of the disciples' fish - but he chose to use some (v.10).
21:15-19	Jesus challenges Peter 3 times. This corresponds to Peter's threefold denial of Jesus.
21:15	The word Jesus uses for love is 'agape' - the love God demonstrates for man. The word Peter uses in response is 'phileo' - the love of man for man.
21:16	Again Jesus uses 'agape' love and Peter responds with 'phileo' love.
21:17	This time Jesus uses 'phileo' love and Peter responds with 'phileo' love. Jesus was prepared to take what Peter had to give and use it.
21:19	'Follow me' - cf. Matthew 1:16-17.

Lesson Plan

Start with a quiz to see what the children have remembered from the previous 4/5 lessons. Split the children into 2 groups. Prior to the lesson write a list of 14-16 questions covering the basic facts of the series.

Make 6 fish for each team (see diagram), using a different colour paper for each set. At the start of the quiz remind the  children that Peter was a fisherman and they are to help him catch fish. Ask the questions of each team alternately. For every right answer pin up an appropriate colour fish. The first team to catch 6 fish wins. If both teams catch 6 fish on the same go the quiz is a draw. Tell the story.

After the story recap on the main things that Peter has learnt about Jesus. Revise the memory verse.

Visual aids

Pictures or flannelgraph. You need Peter, some disciples, a boat trailing a fishing net, a fire with fish cooking.

If you are feeling adventurous you can use models. You require yoghurt pot people for the people, an ice cream container for the boat, 1 empty net (made from a net bought containing oranges or onions), 1 clear plastic bag filled with silver foil fish and a tissue paper

fire with silver foil fish strung above it (see page 69). In order to fill the net with fish, sit behind a table with the plastic bag of fish in your lap. Move the boat to the edge of the table and throw the net over the side onto your lap. Insert the bag of fish into the net and pull it into the boat. This needs a bit of practice but is very effective.

Yoghurt Pot People
Requirements
Yoghurt pots or plastic drinking cups, egg cartons, scraps of material, wool, rubber bands, cotton wool, sellotape, glue, pens.

Instructions
Cut the head from an egg carton and sellotape onto a yoghurt pot or plastic cup. Draw on a face. Dress with a piece of material secured round the middle with wool or a rubber band. Tuck the bottom edge of the material inside the bottom of the pot. Attach the head-dress in similar fashion to the robe. Glue on cotton wool as a beard if required.

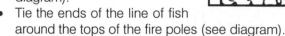

ends together to make a triangular structure (see diagram). Colour the poles and base brown.

- Glue the base of the fire poles to the card base where marked.
- Scrunch up the red tissue paper and glue between the fire poles to make a fire (see diagram).
- Tie the ends of the line of fish around the tops of the fire poles (see diagram).
- Cut out the large oval shape (the stone), colour grey and glue in place on the card base.
- Cut out the 2 loaves of bread and glue on top of the stone.

Activities / 7 - 9s

This activity is a review of the series. Photocopy pages 15 and 70 on paper and page 71 on card for each child.

Instructions
- Cut out the 2 crowns from page 71 and the 6 pictures from the other pages. The crowns are the book covers and the pictures are the pages.
- Put the 6 pictures in the correct order and fill in the missing words.
- Staple the pictures between the 2 crowns on the left hand side to make a book.
- Colour if time permits.

Activities / 3 - 5s

Photocopy page 68 for each child. Each child also requires approximately 10 fish cut from glossy wrapping paper and a rectangle of flame coloured tissue paper. Prior to the lesson, cut out the flames from the picture. The children colour the picture and glue the tissue paper rectangle to the back of the picture, covering the flame holes. The fish are glued onto the net. If you have a net (see visual aids) this can be cut into appropriate sized pieces and glued over the fish.

Activities / 5 - 7s

Each child requires page 69 photocopied on card, a piece of red tissue paper measuring approximately 12 x 9 cm to make the fire, and approximately 20 cm of cotton threaded with 10-12 aluminium foil fish (this needs to be prepared in advance).
- Cut off the bottom section of page 69 to be the base.
- Cut around the fire poles. Fold in half along the dotted line and cut out the centre portion. Fold along the dotted lines at each end and glue the

Jesus knew Peter was really sorry for what he had done.
He gave Peter a special job to do.

cut

Trust in the Lord with all your heart.   Proverbs 3:5

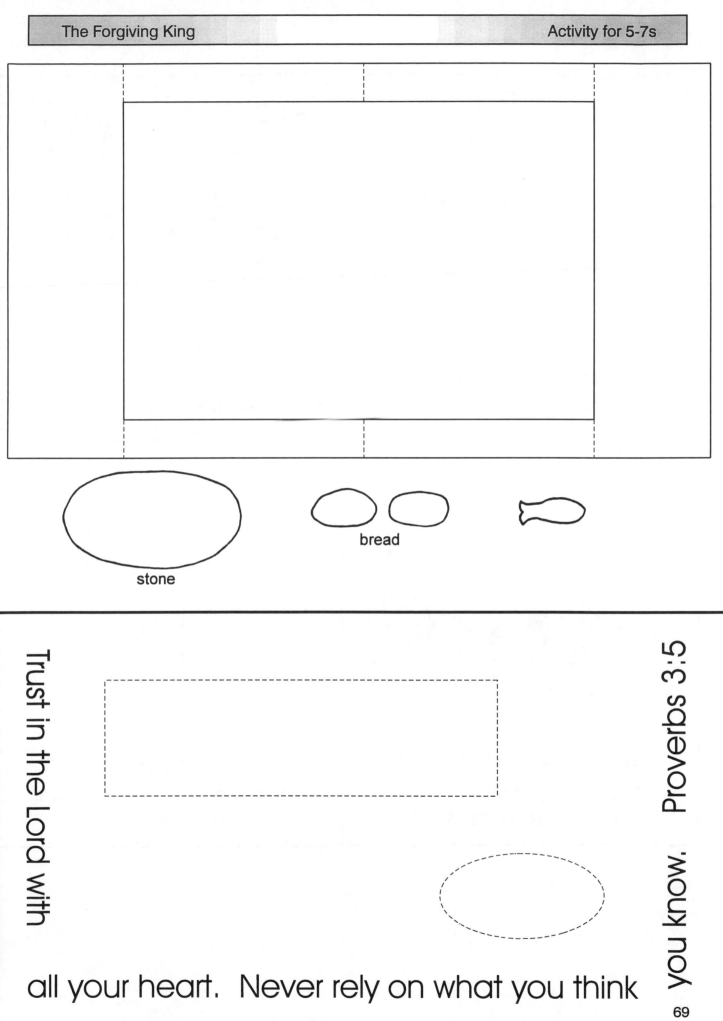

stone

bread

Trust in the Lord with all your heart. Never rely on what you think you know. Proverbs 3:5

Peter learned that Jesus can be

t _ _ _ _ _ _.
(Matthew 14:22-33)

Peter learned about s _ _ _ _ _ _.
(John 13:1-38)

Peter learned about the need to

w _ _ _ _ and p _ _ _.
(Matthew 26:31-58,69-75)

The King was r _ _ _ _ _ _ _.
(John 18:28 - 19:42)

Trust in the Lord with
all your heart.
Never rely on what
you think you know.
Proverbs 3:5

Jesus
the
King

Peter

Week 10	HEALING THE LAME MAN	*Acts 3:1-26*
	To teach the need to have faith in Jesus.	
Week 11	RAISING DORCAS TO LIFE	*Acts 9:31-43*
	To teach that the true response to miracles is belief in the Lord Jesus.	
Week 12	TAKING THE GOSPEL TO THE GENTILES	*Acts 10:1-48*
	To teach that the gospel is for everyone, regardless of race, colour or creed.	
Week 13	IN PRISON	*Acts 12:1-19*
	To teach that God looks after his people in every circumstance.	

Series Aims

1. To understand the stories in their context.

2. To teach the need for each one of us to put our trust in the Lord Jesus.

Peter's first name was Simon (Mark 1:16) and he was given the name Peter (Cephas) by Jesus (John 1:42). Simon Peter had a brother Andrew, who was one of John the Baptist's disciples and who first introduced Peter to Jesus (John 1:35-42). Peter was married (Mark 1:29-31) and subsequently took his wife with him on his missionary journeys (1 Corinthians 9:5). He lived at Capernaum, on the shore of Lake Galilee (Mark 1:21,29) and he and his brother Andrew were fishermen (Mark 1:16). It was whilst he was pursuing his trade that Jesus called him to follow him (Mark 1:16-18). The account of Jesus calling Peter to follow him in Luke 5:1-11 demonstrates that, at this stage, Peter recognised Jesus' authority (he called him 'Master' v.5, and 'Lord' v.8) and also recognised his own sinfulness (v.8). He was prepared to leave home and occupation in order to follow Jesus.

Peter was one of the first disciples to be called by Jesus and heads the list of those 12 who were called to be apostles (Mark 3:13-19). He was one of the 3 disciples who made up the 'inner cabinet' with James and John (Mark 5:35-37; 9:2; 14:32-34). Peter was impulsive (Matthew 14:28-30) and often spoke without thinking (Luke 9:32-33). He had no formal academic training (Acts 4:13), yet was the recognised spokesman for the other disciples (Matthew 16:13-20, Acts 2:14; 3:11-12; 4:5-8).

In the Acts of the Apostles Peter is seen as the leader of the disciples both before and after Pentecost (Acts 1:15ff; 2:14ff). Not only was Peter the spokesman for the disciples, but he was also the one who meted out discipline (Acts 5:1-11). Also he was recognised as one having the power to heal (Acts 5:15-16) and many miracles were performed as part of his ministry. These attested to the fact that Peter was a true follower of God, so that the people would listen to his message (Acts 3:11ff).

When the church spread to Samaria it was Peter and John who were sent to check out the situation and who were used by God to bring the infant church to a full knowledge of Himself (Acts 8:14-17). Peter was also the first apostle to take the gospel to the Gentiles, (Philip was a deacon), after God had demonstrated in a dream that the Gentiles were no longer to be classed as unclean (Acts 10:27-29).

Details of Peter's later life are scanty. Following his miraculous escape from prison in Jerusalem he left for 'another place' (Acts 12:17). He is known to have spent time in Antioch (Galatians 2:11) and probably Corinth, as he had followers there (1 Corinthians 1:12). His first letter is addressed to Christians throughout Asia Minor (1 Peter 1:1) and it is assumed that he had had previous contact with them. The letter was written from Rome (1 Peter 5:13), where his death is thought to have taken place during the persecution of the Christians by Nero.

The first 2 lessons of this series deal with miracles of healing, the third with taking the gospel to the Gentiles, and the fourth with Peter's miraculous escape from prison.

Memory Work

For even the Son of Man did not come to be served, but to serve, and to give his life as a ransom for many.
Mark 10:45

Preparation:
Read Acts 3:1-26, using the Bible study notes to help you.

Lesson aim:
To teach the need to have faith in Jesus.

3:19   'Times of refreshing' refers to the world-wide blessing described by the prophets as being characteristic of the Messianic age (see Joel 2:28-32).

3:22-23   See Deuteronomy 18:15,18-19

3:25   Genesis 22:18 - see also Galatians 3:6-8,14,16.

3:2   The Beautiful gate is thought to have been on the east side of the raised inner area of the Temple - the gate between the court of the women and the court of the Gentiles.
The man was crippled from birth so his legs would have been wasted. This is definitely not a psycho-somatic problem that was cured by the power of suggestion.

3:6   The authority invoked was that of Jesus, cf. v.12-16.

3:11   Solomon's colonnade stretched along the east side of the outer court of the Temple. There were also colonnades stretching along the other 3 sides of the outer court, and all 4 areas were used by the scribes as places to hold their schools and debates. The money-changers and merchants also had their stalls in the colonnades.

3:15   'Author of life' - see John 1:1-3.

3:16   The healing was a sign of Jesus' Messiahship - see Isaiah 35:6.

3:18   See Isaiah 52:13 - 53:12, Mark 10:31-32.

Lesson Plan

Sit the children on the floor and tell them they are not allowed to use their legs, but have to move around by squirming like a fish or pulling themselves along by use of their hands only. Give them simple tasks to perform, e.g. turning round, lying down, sitting up. Increase the severity of the tasks, e.g. the first person to reach a certain place, reaching something on a table. In today's true story from the Bible we will hear about a man who had never been able to walk. Ask the children to listen carefully so that they can tell you at the end who the man met and how he was made better.

At the end of the story go over the answers to the questions and learn the memory verse. The older children can be reminded about the things learnt about Peter in the previous series. How has he changed?

Visual aids

Pictures or flannelgraph. You need Peter, John, the lame man, a crowd of people.

Activities / 3 - 5s

Each child requires page 75 photocopied on card and cotton wool for the beard. Prior to the lesson cut out the 4 pieces and score and fold along the dotted lines on the arms.

- Glue the man's back and front together.
- Cut out the 2 holes at the bottom. (An adult will need to do this.)
- Draw a happy mouth on the face to show how the man felt when he was made better.
- Colour the body and arms.
- Glue on cotton wool for a beard.
- Glue the arms behind the shoulders so that the arms curve forwards.
- Put fingers through the holes at the bottom to act as legs. The man sits down with legs in front. When he is healed he jumps up and walks.
- Repeat the story with the children using their figures to act it out.

Activities / 5 - 7s

Make a pop-up card. Photocopy the man at the bottom of this page, and pages 76 and 77 back to back for each child.

- Fold the double-sided page in half with the kneeling man on the front and the memory verse on the back.
- Colour both sides of the double-sided page and the figure of the man.
- Cut out the box containing the man. Fold it in half with the man on the **outside**. Fold the side flaps back.
- Glue the side flaps to the inside of the double-sided page along the marked lines. When the card is opened the figure of the lame man walking should pop up.

Activities / 7 - 9s

Make a decoder. Photocopy pages 78 and 79 for each child. Follow the instructions on page 78.

Teacher's Challenge Solution

pages 6, 22, 28, 42, 47, 60, plus one in weeks 11-13.

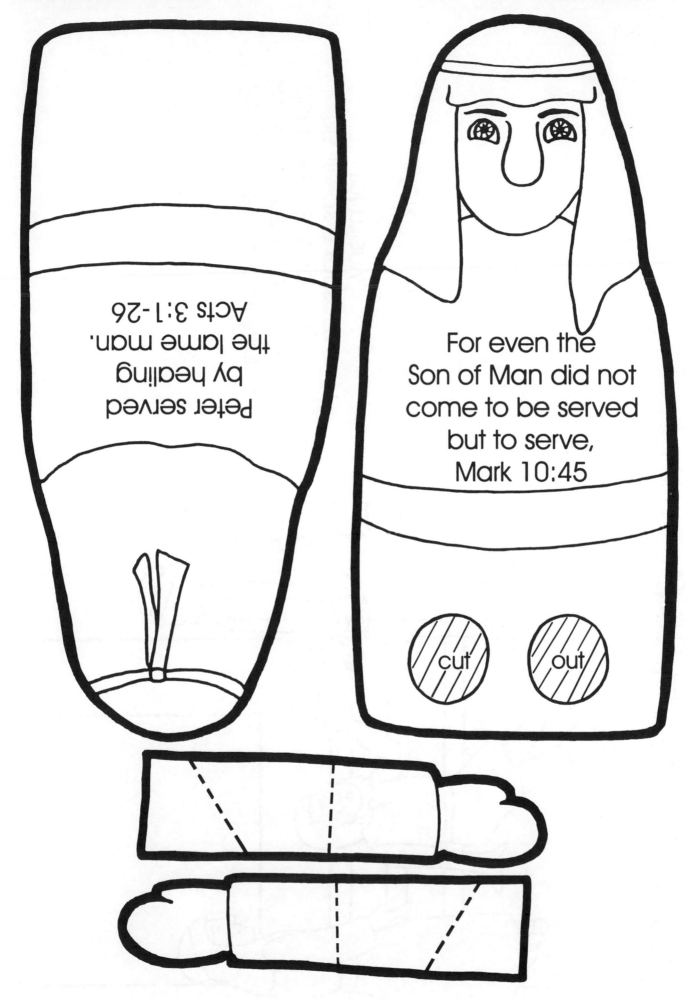

For even the
Son of Man did not
come to be served
but to serve,
Mark 10:45

cut   out

Peter served
by healing
the lame man.
Acts 3:1-26

For even the Son of Man
did not come to be served
but to serve, and to give
his life as a ransom
for many.

Mark 10:45

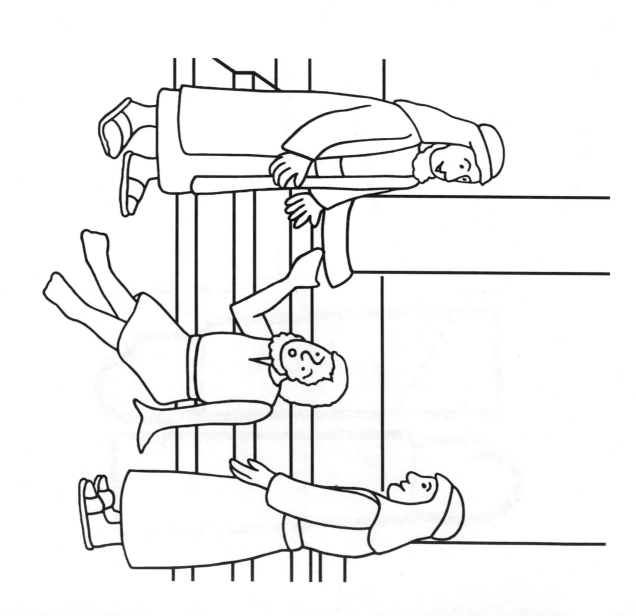

Peter said, "I have no money, but I give
you what I have. In the name of Jesus ...."

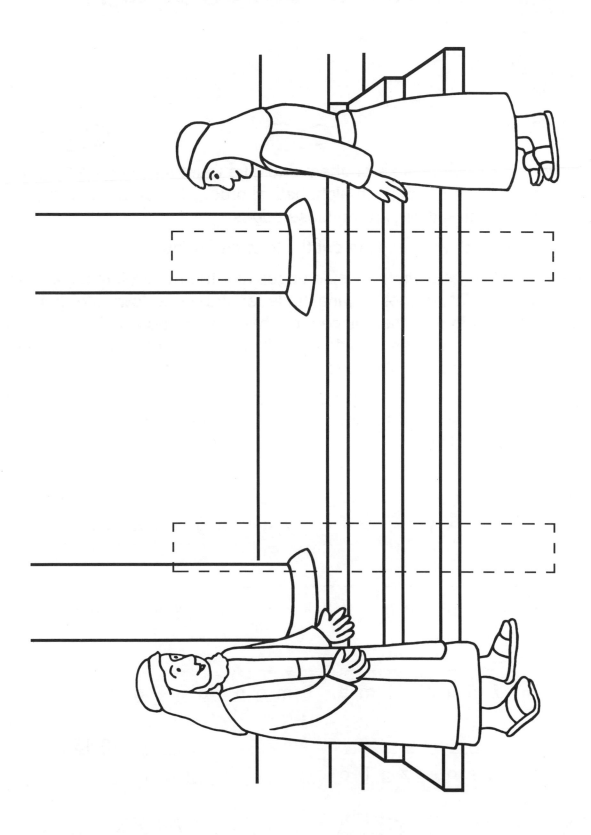

"Get up and walk!"

Make a foot decoder.

1. Cut off the 3 strips with letters on them and glue together to make 1 long strip with the top line of letters in alphabetical order. Sellotape over the joins back and front so that there are no loose edges.

2. Cut out the 2 foot shapes and cut out the 2 holes on foot A.

3. Put glue on foot A between the 2 side edges and the dotted lines. Do **not** glue between the dotted lines. Place the letter strip face down along the unglued section of foot A, then place the other foot on top sticking the 2 foot shapes together. The letters should be visible through the 2 holes on the foot and the letter strip should move freely through the foot.

4. Decode the memory verse by pulling the letter strip through the foot until the letter to decode appears in the bottom hole. The letter visible in the top hole is the letter to write down.

_ _ _   _ _ _ _   _ _ _   _ _ _   _ _   _ _ _   _ _ _   _ _ _

q v o   n u n i   x y n   e v i   v q   z g i   k m k   i v x

_ _ _ _   _ _   _ _   _ _ _ _ _   _ _ _   _ _   _ _ _ _ _

t v z n   x v   d n   e n o u n k   d l x   x v   e n o u n

_ _ _   _ _   _ _ _ _   _ _ _   _ _ _ _   _ _   _

g i k   x v   f m u n   y m e   b m q n   g e   g

_ _ _ _ _ _   _ _ _   _ _ _ _.   _ _ _ _ 10:45

o g i e v z   q v o   z g i c   z g o r

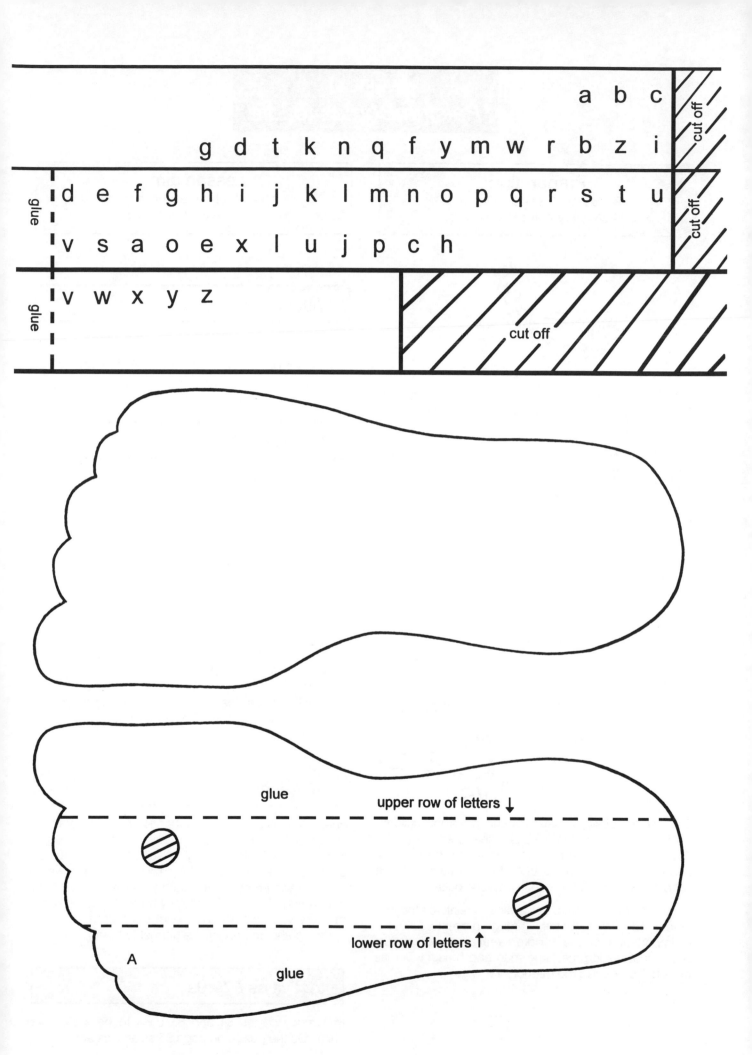

a b c

g d t k n q f y m w r b z i

cut off

glue
d e f g h i j k l m n o p q r s t u

v s a o e x l u j p c h

cut off

glue
v w x y z

cut off

glue

upper row of letters ↓

lower row of letters ↑

A

glue

WEEK 11
Raising Dorcas to Life

Lesson aim:
To teach that the true response to miracles is belief in the Lord Jesus.

9:31   The church had spread into Samaria (see Acts 1:8), due to persecution by the Jewish authorities.

9:35   Sharon is the coastal plain.

9:36   Joppa is the modern Jaffa. It is a sea-port serving Jerusalem, which is about 35 miles away to the south-east. Lydda is on the road between Joppa and Jerusalem and is about 11 miles from Joppa.
Tabitha (Aramaic) and Dorcas (Greek) mean 'gazelle'.

9:39   Dorcas had used her gifts to help the church.

9:42   The right response to a miracle is belief in Jesus (John 20:30-31).

Lesson Plan

Start by discussing what happens when the children are ill. What does Mummy do? What does the doctor do? You need a thermometer, an empty pill bottle, a bandage, etc. In today's true story from the Bible we will discover how Peter made someone better.

At the end of the story use the aids to reinforce the way Peter made Dorcas better - through prayer to Jesus. It is important that the children realise it was Jesus' power that healed the lame man and brought Dorcas back to life. Revise the memory verse.

Visual aids

Thermometer, empty pill bottle, bandage, etc.

Pictures with a movable Dorcas (see activity for 3-5s).

A map for the older children to show Peter's journey.

Activities / 3 - 5s

Photocopy pages 81 and 82 for each child. Prior to the lesson cut out the rectangle containing people and the 2 pieces of Dorcas. If possible glue the pieces of Dorcas onto card as this gives a better result. Cut along the thick black lines of the doors so that they can be folded back along the dotted lines to open. Each child requires 2 split pin paper fasteners.
* Colour the picture, the people and Dorcas.
* Glue the rectangle of people behind the doors so that the people are visible when the doors are opened.
* Attach the upper part of Dorcas in front of the lower half, using a split pin paper fastener through the dots.
* Attach Dorcas' feet to the picture using a split pin paper fastener at X. Dorcas can lie down, sit up and stand up.

Activities / 5 - 7s

Photocopy page 83 on card for each child. Prior to the lesson cut out the card garments for those children who have difficulty managing scissors. Use a hole punch to make a hole at the neck of each garment at X. The children colour the garments then thread them onto a ring binder or length of wool in the order of the memory verse. If using a length of wool tie the two ends together to prevent the garments falling off.

Activities / 7 - 9s

Photocopy pages 84 and 85 back to back for each child. Do the puzzle on page 85 as a class activity.

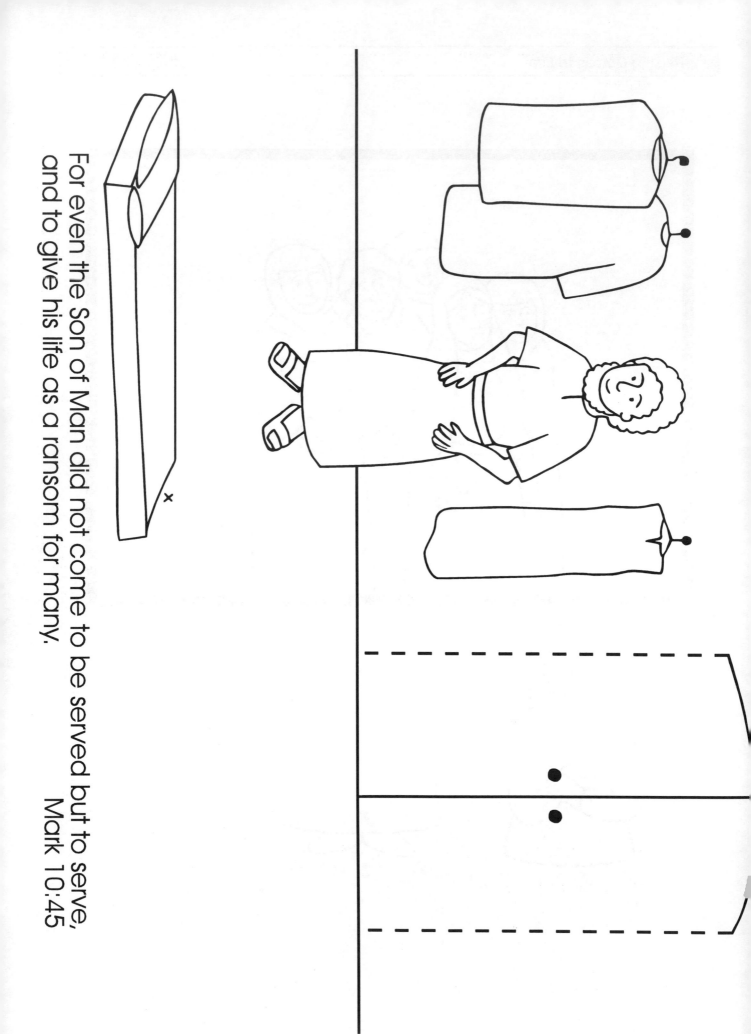

For even the Son of Man did not come to be served but to serve,
and to give his life as a ransom for many.

Mark 10:45

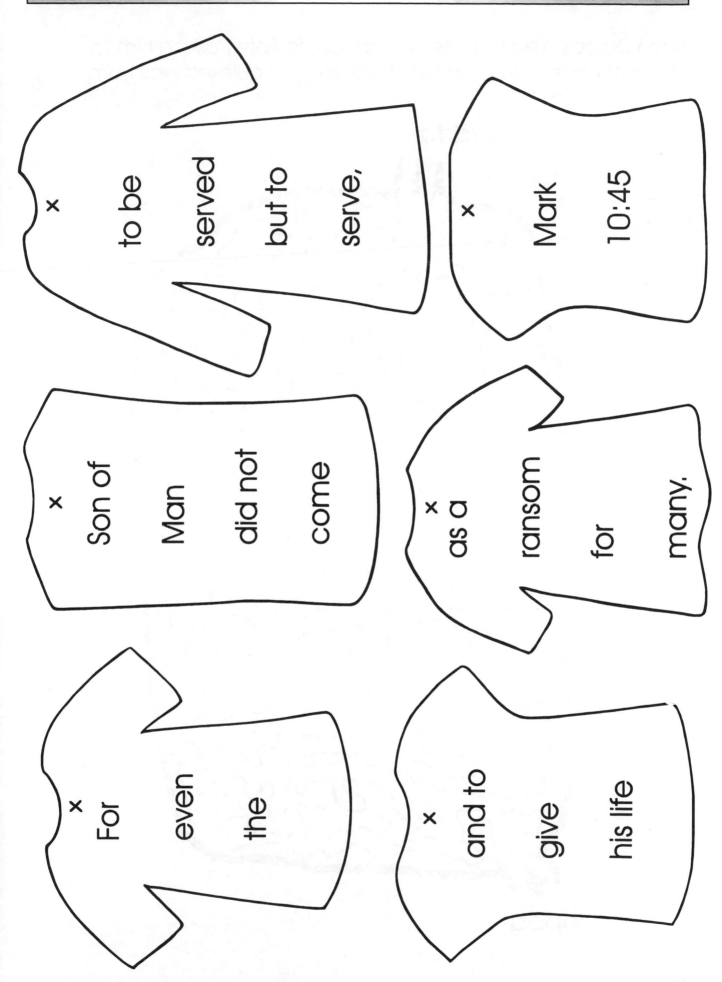

to be
served
but to
serve,

Mark
10:45

Son of
Man
did not
come

as a
ransom
for
many.

For
even
the

and to
give
his life

When Dorcas died a message was sent to Peter, asking him to come at once. Can you help Peter find the quickest way from Lydda to Joppa?

Lydda

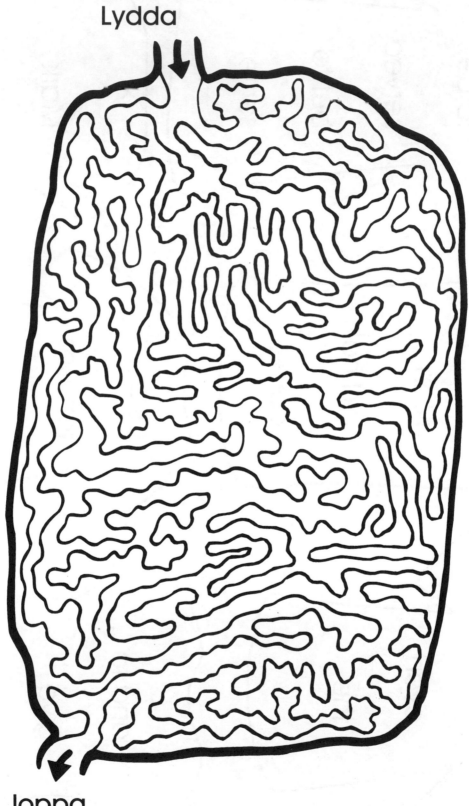

Joppa

GNB, NIV, KJV

What did Jesus come to do? Using the Bible to help you, answer the questions from the passage and place your answers in the grid below. The column indicated by the arrow will provide the answer. The story is found in the book of Acts. The numbers in brackets tell you what chapter and verse to look up.

1. What was Tabitha's other name? (9:36)

2. What happened to Dorcas? (9:37)

3. Where was the room where Dorcas was laid? (9:39)

4. Who did Peter call in to see that Dorcas was alive? (9:41 - GNB, NIV)
    (KJV - the required word is another word for 'saints' beginning with B.)

5. What was Simon's job? (9:43)

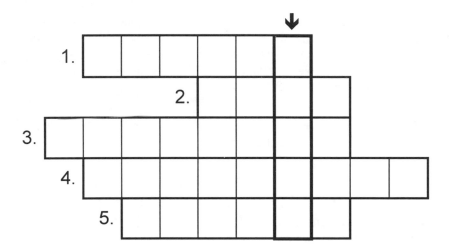

For even the Son of Man did not come to be served but to _ _ _ _ _ ,
and to give his life as a ransom for many.
Mark 10:45

Lesson aim:
To teach that the gospel is for everyone,
regardless of race, colour or creed.

10:1   Caesarea is a major port on the Mediterranean Sea. It was built by Herod the Great and was the place where the Roman Governor had his principal residence. It was situated about 32 miles north of Joppa.

10:2   God-fearers were those Gentiles who subscribed to the Jewish faith but did not become proselytes and were not circumcised.

10:4   Memorial offering - see Leviticus 2:2-3.

10:6   A tanner dealt with dead animals, so would have been shunned by orthodox Jews.

10:12-14   See Leviticus 11:1-47 for the Jewish food laws.

10:23   Peter took 6 people with him (Acts 11:12).

10:30   4 days ago -
day 1   Cornelius received his vision.
day 2   Peter received his vision and Cornelius' messengers arrived.
day 3   Peter sets out for Caesarea.
day 4   Peter arrives at Caesarea.

10:34   God shows no favouritism - see also Deuteronomy 10:17, Romans 2:11, Ephesians 6:9. This was an amazing thought for Peter, who had been brought up to believe that all non-Jews were to be despised. The children need to be reminded that God is the same today and accepts anyone who comes to him through faith in Jesus Christ. For the older children the teacher needs to have examples of the type of person the children would find unacceptable.

10:38   Refers to Jesus' baptism.

10:41   Emphasises the fact of Jesus' bodily resurrection.

10:43   See Isaiah 53.

10:46   See Acts 11:15 - the speaking in other tongues was the same as the disciples experienced at Pentecost.

Lesson Plan

Start by recapping on the previous 2 lessons using a question and answer format. Peter was learning how to serve Jesus. Remind the children that the healing miracles resulted in people listening to the message and believing in Jesus (Acts 3: 10-12; 4:4; 9:42). Peter

wanted people to believe in Jesus, but only the people from his own country. In today's true story from the Bible we will find out how God showed Peter that he wanted people from every country to hear about Jesus and believe in him. Ask the children to listen carefully so that they can tell you the name of the man Peter was sent to, what country he was from, and how God showed Peter it was right to tell him about Jesus.

At the end of the story go over the three questions and revise the memory verse.

Visual aids

Pictures or flannelgraph. You need Peter, Cornelius, an angel, messengers (optional), the sheet with animals, birds and reptiles. You might want to enlarge and colour the activity for 3-5s to use for the first part of the story.

A map is useful for the older children to show Peter's journey.

Activities / 3 - 5s

Photocopy pages 88, 89 and 90 for each child. Prior to the lesson cut slits where marked on the picture page. Cut the top from page 89 to make a tab. Cut out the sheet on page 89 along the thick black line and fold it along the dotted line. Roughly cut out the figures on page 88, fold each one along the dotted line and cut out properly along the thick black line.
- Colour the picture and the birds and animals.
- Glue both halves of the birds and animals together.
- Fold the cut out sheet in half along the dotted line and glue the sides together to make a pocket, leaving the top open. Glue the tab behind the bottom of the sheet where indicated (see diagram).

- Thread the tab through the slits so that the sheet is out of sight above and behind the picture and the line across the centre of the tab lines up with the line between the walls on the picture. Place the coloured figures in the sheet. When the tab is pulled down the sheet descends in front of Peter. The children can pull out the birds and animals to show the types that were not to be eaten.

Activities / 5 - 7s

Photocopy pages 91 and 92 for each child. Prior to the lesson cut along the thick black lines around the doors and fold back along the dotted lines. Cut off the strip at the bottom of page 91, fold in half and cut out 2 locking bars.
- Colour both pages.
- Glue the 2 locking bars together back to back.
- Put a split pin paper fastener through the dot on the right hand door. Attach the locking bar to the left hand door at the dot with another split pin paper fastener. The locking bar can be brought down to rest on the right hand side split pin to keep the doors shut.
- Glue page 91 behind page 92, only gluing at the sides so that the doors can be opened to show the people. Ask the children to open the doors to see who Jesus came to save.

Activities / 7 - 9s

Photocopy page 93 for each child. Discuss with the children why taking the good news of Jesus to Gentiles was a new idea for Peter (see Bible study notes on 10:34). Who are the people we find unacceptable today? For children this may not be tramps, but people who break the law, e.g. murderers, paedophiles, burglars, etc.

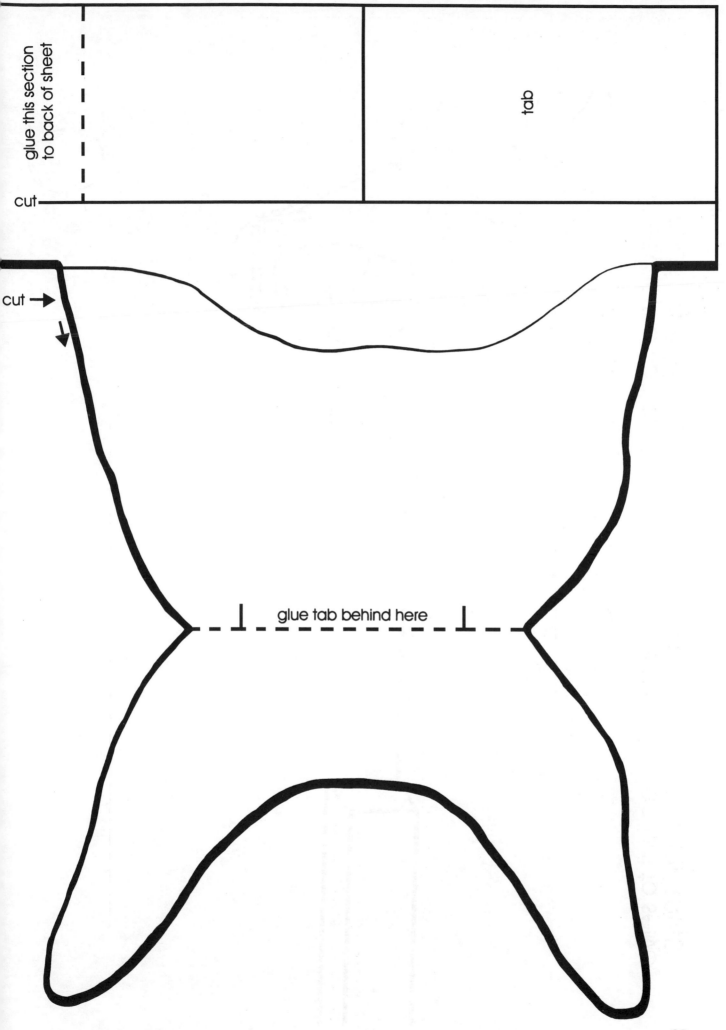

glue this section to back of sheet

cut

tab

cut →

glue tab behind here

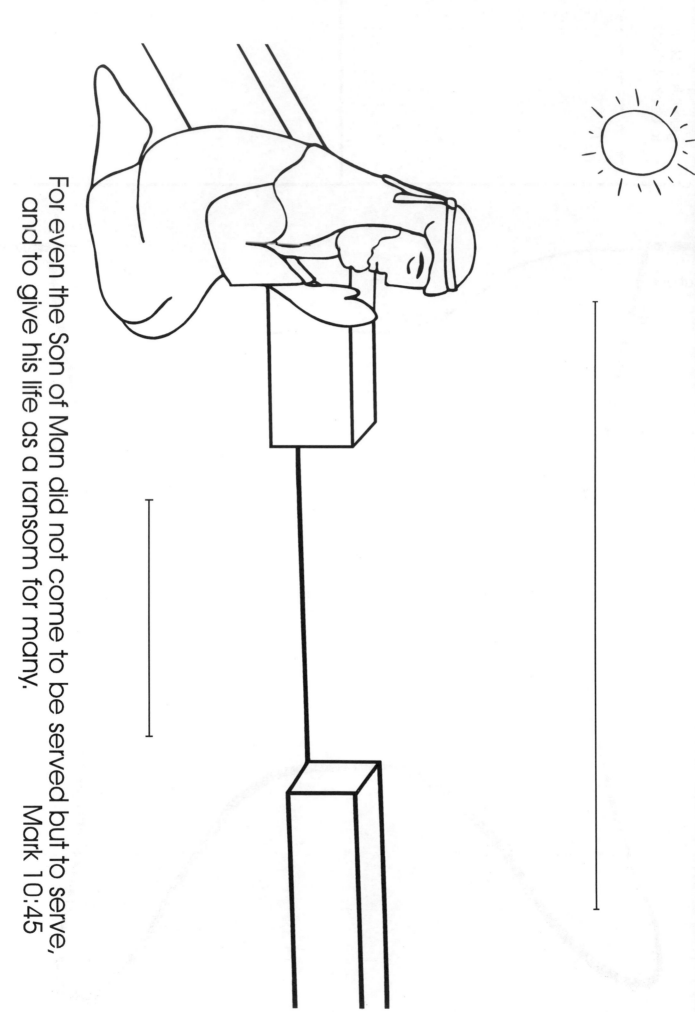

For even the Son of Man did not come to be served but to serve, and to give his life as a ransom for many.

Mark 10:45

all

people

For even the Son of Man did not come to be served but to serve, and to give his life as a ransom for many.

Mark 10:45

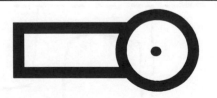

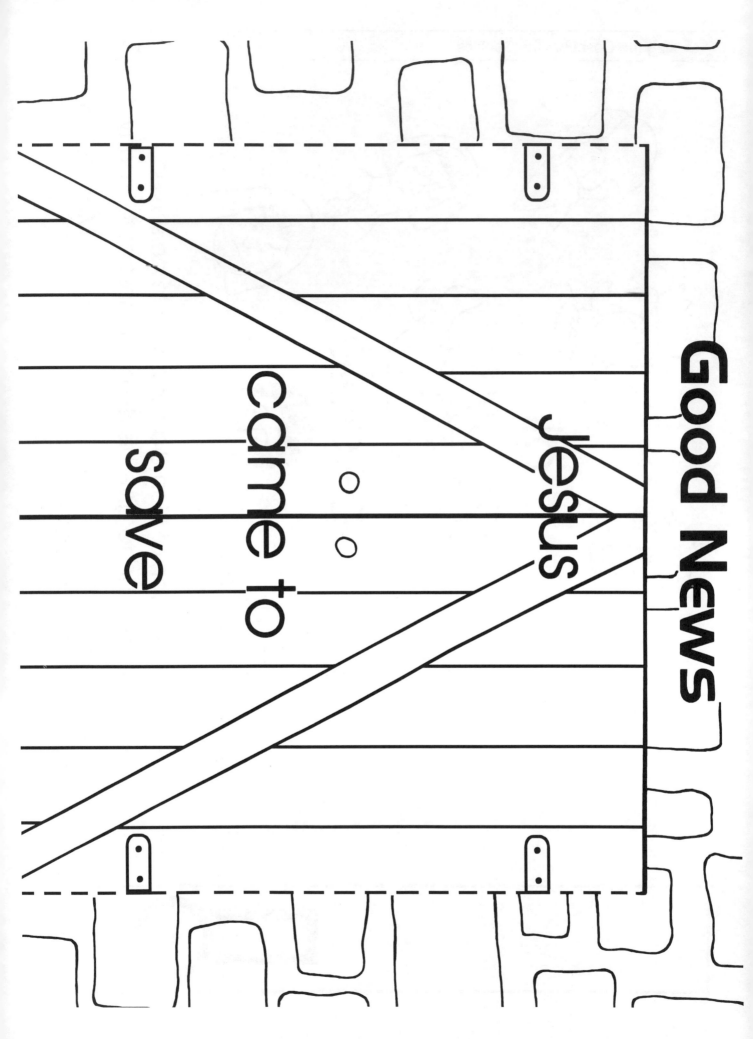

Jesus came to save

Good News

Taking the Gospel to the Gentiles

Acts 10:1-46

Peter went to Caesarea to see Cornelius.
Colour all the dotted shapes to discover something about Cornelius.

Peter learned that the good news about Jesus Christ is for all people - Jews and Gentiles.

For even the Son of Man did not come to be served but to serve, and to give his life as a ransom for many.
Mark 10:45

Preparation:
Read Acts 12:1-19, using the Bible study notes to help you.

Lesson aim:
To teach that God looks after his people in every circumstance.

The context of this story is found in Acts 11:19-30. Paul and Barnabas went up to Jerusalem at least 14 years after Paul's conversion (Galatians 2:1-14).

12:1   Herod Agrippa was the grandson of Herod the Great (Luke 1:5). He ruled over Judea from AD 41-44. His sudden death in AD 44 is recorded in Acts 12:21-23. He was, despite his Edomite origin, a patron of the Jewish faith and sought to maintain friendly relations with the Jewish religious leaders (v.3).

12:3   Feast of Unleavened Bread = Passover.

12:4   There was 1 squad of soldiers for each watch period (3 hours). 1 squad consisted of 4 soldiers, 2 in the cell with Peter and 2 on guard outside (v.6).

12:17   James, the half-brother of Jesus, was now head of the church, following the execution of James, son of Zebedee.

Lesson Plan

Start by discussing with the children what they do when they are in situations that make them unhappy, e.g. friend or sibling taking their toys off them, being bullied, afraid of the dark, etc. Who do they go to for help? Why? Before the story starts make sure that they realise that they go for help to the person they know can help them.

At the end of the story revise the things Peter has been learning about what it means to serve Jesus. Revise the memory verse.

Visual aids

Either use pictures or peg people (see instructions on page 61). Plaited wool/string makes good chains. You need Peter, 4 soldiers and the angel.

Photocopy pages 96 and 97 for each child. Prior to the lesson cut 4 slits where marked on the picture page. Cut the slider containing Peter and the angel from page 96.

- Colour the picture and the slider.
- Thread the slider through the picture, starting from the back. Start with Peter in chains. Pull the slider towards the right to show Peter released from his chains.

Photocopy pages 98 and 99 on card for each child. Prior to the lesson cut off the strip containing Peter and the angel and fold along the dotted line. Cut out the figures leaving them joined at the head. Cut out the prison from page 99. Cut out the window and the section beneath the gates. Cut up the centre and along the top of the gates as far as the dotted lines. Score along all dotted lines. Cut out the bar for the gate and the window bars and place in an envelope for each child with Peter and the angel.

Instructions

- Colour Peter and the angel. Glue the back and front together leaving the bottom tabs free. Fold the tabs outwards and glue to the marked area on the base sheet with the figures facing the entrance.
- Cut out the 3 bars and glue them vertically to the inside of the prison window.
- Make a hole in the gate at the dot and cut a small slit where marked on the other gate. ⊢⊣ (An adult will need to do this.)
- Fold the prison along the dotted lines. The bottom tabs on all 4 walls fold **outwards**. The gates fold outwards.
- Glue the side tabs of the prison inside the end walls to make a box.
- Take the bar for the gate, score and fold along the dotted line. Glue the 2 halves together. Make a hole at the dot. Attach the bar to the left gate using a split pin paper fastener through the dots. Make sure that the bar moves freely on the gate. Sellotape the ends of the split pin to the inside of the gate.
- Insert a paper clip through the other gate with the shorter end on the outside pointing upwards (see diagram). Sellotape the longer end to the inside of the gate. When the gates are closed the locking bar can be swung over and slotted into the end of the paper clip to secure the gate (see diagram).
- Glue the prison onto the base sheet where marked with the tabs sticking out. The backs of Peter and the angel can be seen through the window and their fronts can be seen when the gate is opened.

Photocopy page 100 and the armour on this page for each child.

- Cut out the pieces of armour from this page. (This can be done in advance to save time.)
- Go through Ephesians 6:10-18, discuss each piece of armour and glue it onto the soldier. (The outline of the shield is marked by dotted lines.)
- Ephesians 6:18 states that it must all be put on with prayer. Write 'Prayer' over the top of the soldier and join the 2 ends of 'Prayer' with a line that encircles the soldier.

God cared for Peter in difficult circumstances (prison). Whereas God took Peter out of prison, he does not always deliver us from difficult situations. Discuss how God's armour helps us to stand firm.

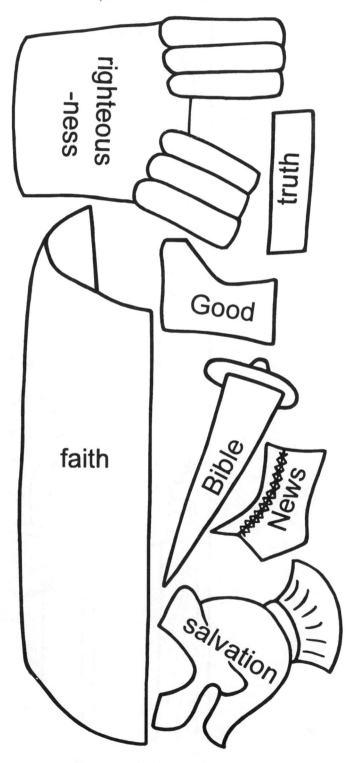

Peter in Prison

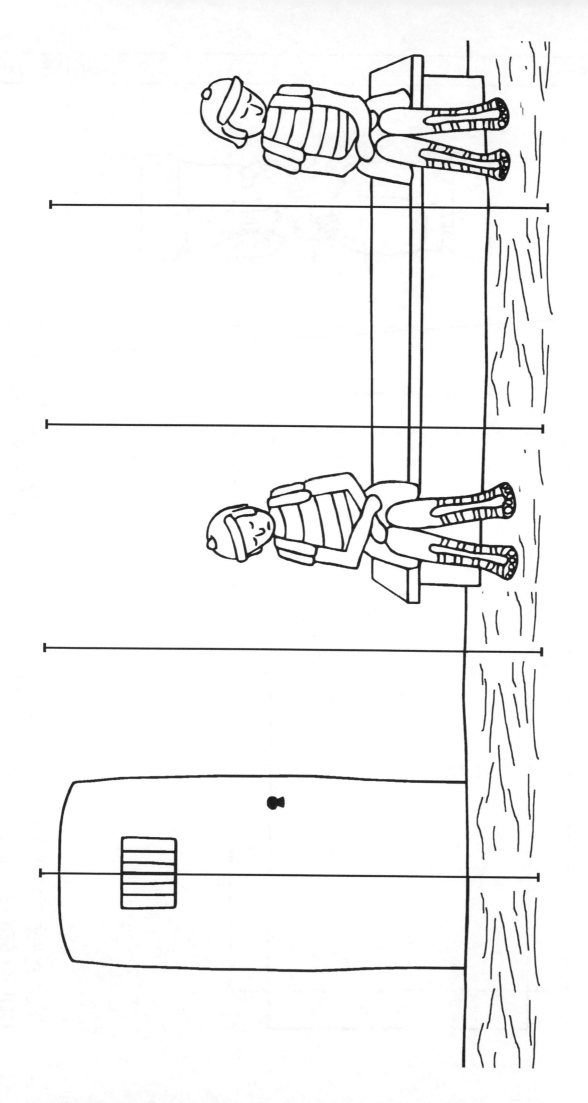

For even the Son of Man did not come to be served but to serve,
and to give his life as a ransom for many.
Mark 10:45

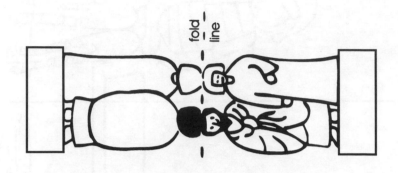

fold line

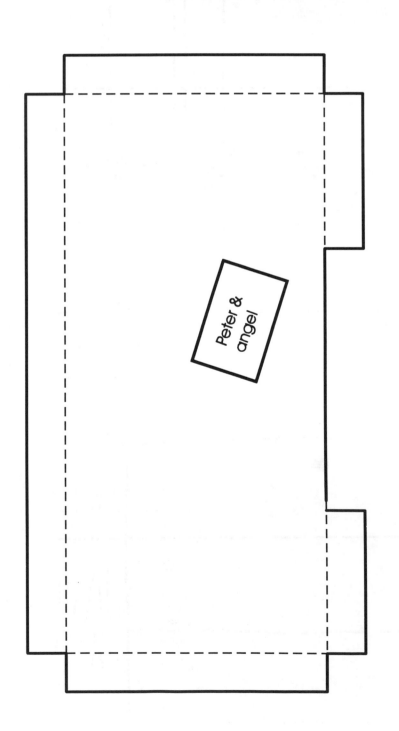

Peter & angel

For even the Son of Man did not come to be served but to serve, and to give his life as a ransom for many.
Mark 10:45

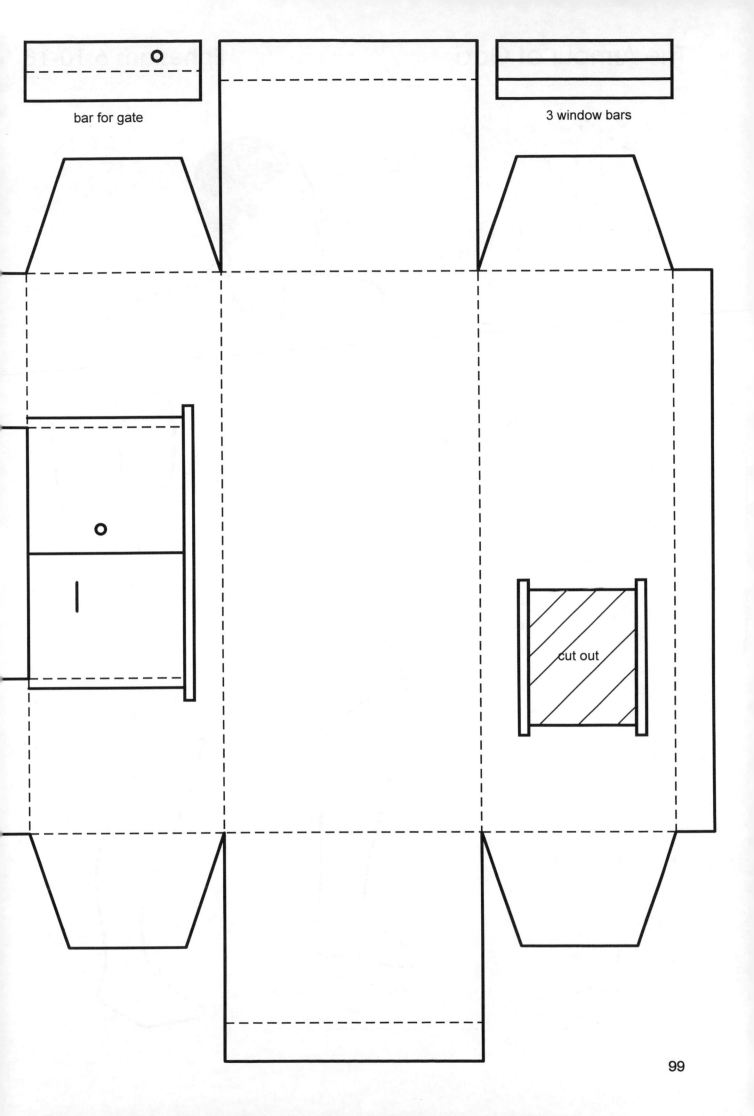

bar for gate

3 window bars

cut out

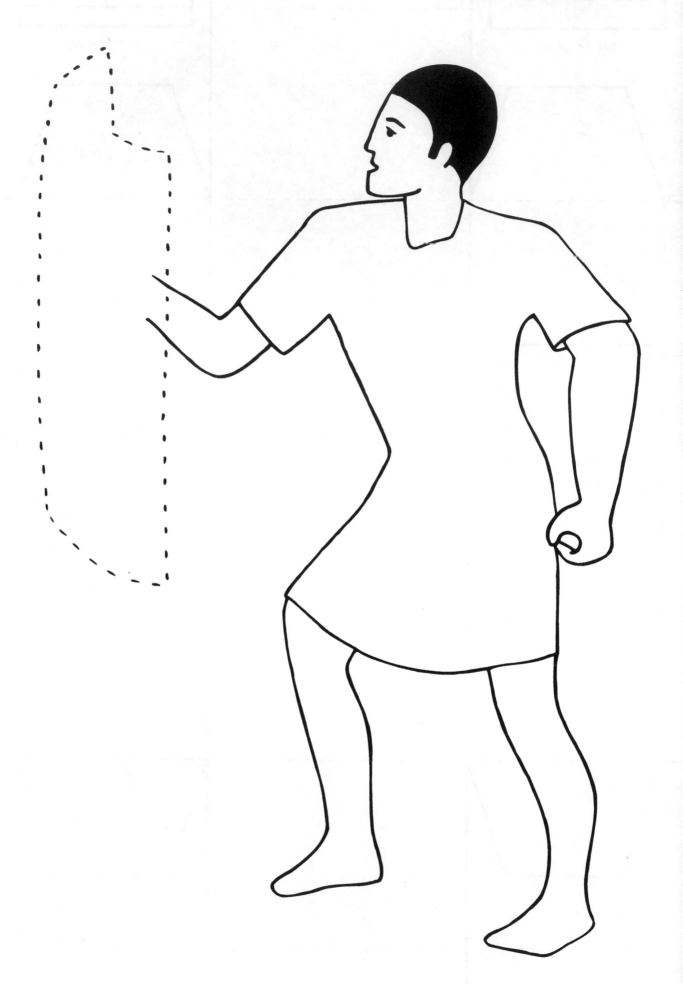